MW01198837

The Baby Manual

The Baby Manual

The Ultimate Guide for New Parents

Second edition

written by
Carole Keim, MD

The Baby Manual
ISBN-10: 1977608698

Notice

Knowledge and best practice in this field are constantly changing and being updated. As new research and experience becomes available, changes in practice, treatment, and advice may become necessary or appropriate. Readers are advised to check the most current information to verify the validity of advice given in this book. It is the responsibility of parents, relying on their own experience and knowledge, to take the best care of their children, and take all appropriate safety precautions. To the fullest extent of the law, neither the author nor the publishers assume any liability for any injury or damage to persons or property arising out of or related to any use of the material contained in this book.

The Baby Manual: The Ultimate Guide for New Parents / by Carole Keim MD. — 2nd ed.
ISBN-13: 978-1977608697

Self-published by the author

Printed in the United States of America

*This book is dedicated to
my daughter, Anya.*

*She is the inspiration for the
second edition.*

Table of Contents

A Note from
the Author

Did you ever wish new babies came with a manual? You're not alone.

As a pediatrician, I have the opportunity to meet with many families for their newborn appointments. I started *The Baby Manual* after several parents mentioned to me that they felt comfortable caring for their baby in the hospital with the nurses around, but once they got home they felt totally lost. Many parents were blindsided by the things their child was doing, and they weren't sure what was normal and what wasn't. I can't even tell you how many parents told me outright, "I wish this baby came with a manual!"

The information in *The Baby Manual* is based on 15 years of accumulation of pediatric knowledge. This book is designed to provide the standard information that a doctor would give at the first several newborn and infant checkups.

I have a baby of my own now, and I know how overwhelming it is to be a new parent. My baby was born after the first edition of The Baby Manual, so after having her I kept notes of all the information I wish I'd had before she was born, and added all of it to the second edition.

I have tried to keep *The Baby Manual* informative and concise. If you would like more information, you will find a list of references with books, articles, and websites to support and expand upon all of the information in this book.

While this book makes many generalizations, I am aware that no two families or babies are the same. This book was written with the average American family in mind, and I am not trying to offend anyone. So for example, when I use terms like "mom/dad" you may substitute in names of other caregivers, and when I refer to the hospital birth, I realize that many families choose to give birth at home or at a birth center. I kept all references to babies gender-neutral, except when referring to genitalia.

Every baby is different, and some babies are normal without being average. The information in this book is not intended to replace the advice of your pediatrician or family doctor, who knows your baby personally. I wrote this book with the knowledge I have amassed as a pediatrician, to advise the majority of the population. If your doctor gives you different advice, please follow it.

I hope you enjoy *The Baby Manual, Second Edition*!

- Carole Keim, MD
Board certified pediatrician

What's New in the Second Edition

- More photos and diagrams
- Updates to guidelines and recommendations
- Additional information on breastfeeding
- An extra section at the end of the germs chapter with signs that your baby might be sick
- A chapter about circumcision
- A section in the peeing/pooping chapter about potty training from birth and elimination communication
- A chapter about postpartum depression and other postpartum mood disorders
- Information on how and when to start solid foods
- Information about teething
- An index for quick reference
- Myths/facts have been changed to frequently asked questions
- List of baby items to purchase before and after baby is born
- List of what to pack in the diaper bag
- Chart to track baby's eating, sleeping, and peeing/pooping

Chapter 1

Essential Information Before Your Baby Arrives

Congratulations, you're having a baby! Have you ever wondered what will happen during the delivery? This chapter outlines what you can expect on your big day.

How to Tell You're in Labor

You probably have most preparations in place by now - baby items, a possible name picked out, and so on. But do you know how to tell when you're in active labor? It's not as obvious as you would think.

Your contractions will start off pretty infrequently, then get stronger and more frequent as you get closer to the time of delivery. It takes about one contraction every 5 minutes to actually cause your cervix to start dilating, and it usually takes several hours to dilate the full 10 centimeters. Some birth professionals use the 3-1-1 rule: you should head to the hospital when you have contractions every 3 minutes, lasting 1 minute each, for 1 hour.

If your water breaks, you should go to the hospital. There will be a big gush of fluid, and it will continue to leak until your baby is born. The fluid will soak through your underwear and down to your knees, if not to your socks. If you aren't sure whether your water has broken, it's better to go in and get checked. The hospital staff can do a quick test.

Things to Bring to the Hospital

It's a good idea to pack a small hospital bag a few weeks before your due date. If you don't have the bag packed and you are in labor, don't worry about it! They have everything you need at the hospital. But if you are able to prepare ahead of time, here are some items you might like to have with you:

- An outfit for you to wear home. Your belly takes a few months to shrink to pre-pregnancy size, so bring maternity clothes. Remember to pack a nursing bra and breast pads!

- A few outfits for your baby. Don't forget a hat and socks, and a blanket to wrap baby in.

- A car seat to bring baby home in. The hospital won't let you leave without it. If you forget it at home, a family member can always bring it to you later.

- A toiletry bag with your favorite items (shampoo, soap, lotion, toothbrush, deodorant, and makeup).

- Maxi pads (super/overnight absorbency) and 3-4 pairs of underwear. You will bleed a lot after the delivery, even if you have a C-section. The maxi pads at the hospital work fine, but they are long and thick and don't have adhesive on the back, so you may feel like you have a huge pillow jostling around in your underwear. You won't be allowed to use tampons or a menstrual cup for 6 weeks after delivery.

- Pajamas, slippers, and extra socks. They will probably be more comfortable than those provided by the hospital.

- A phone (and a camera if you have one), and the charger(s).

- Hard candies to suck on during labor (since you're not allowed to eat anything) and high-protein snacks and a water bottle for after the delivery.

- Something to help pass the time - a book, tablet, laptop, movies, music, etc.

- A breast pump if you have one, so you can practice with the lactation specialists in the hospital.

- A written list of any medications you take regularly.

Do NOT bring:

- Jewelry, watches, and anything else that is expensive and might get lost. Remember you will be there for a few days in several rooms (labor/delivery room, postpartum/maternity room, possibly also an operating room and recovery room).

- Any tobacco or drug products. You will not be allowed to go outside to use them for the duration of your stay. The hospital can give you a nicotine patch if you need one.

- Children less than 12 years old, especially during flu season (October - March). School-age children are the most likely age group to inadvertently pass germs onto a newborn baby. Many hospitals have a policy that does not allow children in the maternity ward. If children do visit, make sure they wash their hands with soap and water before touching the new baby. If you want your child to be present during the delivery, check with the hospital staff beforehand to make sure it's ok.

The Delivery Staff

There are going to be a whole lot of people in your room for the delivery. The following people are likely to be present:

- An obstetrician or midwife

- One or two delivery nurses

- A pediatric nurse

- A pediatrician or family doctor for the baby

- Your partner (spouse, birth coach, etc.)

- Any family members that you allow

- Other people of your choosing (such as a doula)

What the Pediatrician and Nurses are Doing

Shortly after delivery, your baby will be examined by the pediatrician and/or pediatric nurse (typically across the room, but sometimes in another room). This is what happens during that first exam:

- Your baby is taken to a warmer and dried off. It's very important that your baby doesn't get cold, and babies can lose heat very fast because they come out wet with amniotic fluid. I'm sure you know how quickly you get cold when stepping out of the tub if you don't have a towel!

- The doctor examines your baby for APGAR scores. Each of the 5 components of the APGAR score (Appearance, Pulse, Grimace, Activity, Respirations) can be given 0, 1, or 2 points. The APGAR scores are checked when your baby is 1 minute old and 5 minutes old, and they tell the doctor how well your baby is making the transition to the outside world. An APGAR score that is 7 or higher is a good score.

- The nurse will measure your baby's length and head circumference. Then the nurse stamps footprints of your baby onto a paper, for identification. She will write down all of the medical information needed for your baby's birth certificate. Some hospitals will weigh your baby right away, while others will weigh your baby later in the nursery.

- The nurse will give your baby eye ointment. The eye ointment is to protect your baby from getting pink eye (conjunctivitis) from the bacteria that live in the vaginal canal. Even babies born by C-section can be exposed to these bacteria, since the bacteria can travel into the amniotic fluid. The ointment mostly protects against the two worst kinds of pink eye - those caused by gonorrhea and chlamydia - but will help protect against other bacteria as well. Since it's possible for a woman to have an infection without any symptoms, it's a good idea to give the ointment to your baby preventatively.

- The nurse will give your baby a Vitamin K injection to prevent bleeding. All babies are born with just enough Vitamin K-dependent clotting factors to last for the first 5-7 days. After that time, when the clotting factors are used up, babies can bleed spontaneously. This is called hemorrhagic disease of the newborn. They can get nosebleeds, bloody stools, and even bleed into their brain (a stroke). The amount of Vitamin K that babies are able to absorb orally (either in breast milk, formula, or oral vitamin supplements) is not enough to prevent this from happening, so every baby needs a Vitamin K injection.

Weight Loss, then Weight Gain

Your baby will lose a few ounces over the first few days in the hospital, and this is totally normal. Most of the weight loss is water weight (from no longer being immersed in amniotic fluid), and some is from your baby performing the exhausting tasks of eating, digesting, and crying. It typically takes 7-14 days for babies to return to their birthweight. After regaining birth weight, babies should gain about one ounce every 1-2 days for the first few weeks.

The Newborn Screen

When your baby is at least 24 hours old, the nurse will take a blood sample from your baby's heel. If you have ever had a fingerstick blood test, it is kind of like that, except babies' fingers are too small to stick, so the heel is used. The nurse will put about 5 drops of your baby's blood onto a piece of paper, which gets mailed into the state health department. They will test your baby's blood for rare and obscure (and mostly unpronounceable!) genetic disorders. Each state tests for 31 "core" diseases, and then up to 27 "optional" diseases. The optional diseases are chosen by the state based on the genetic composition of the state residents and how likely they are to be found in a newborn. The results will be sent to your pediatrician.

Choosing a pediatrician

Most hospitals will require you to set a follow-up appointment with a pediatrician before you go home with your new baby. You should choose a pediatrician before your baby is born, if at all possible. Many pediatricians offer appointments for a meet-and-greet, so you can see if they are a good fit for your family.

Remember, not all pediatricians are the same, just like not all people are the same. Choosing the right one for your family can depend on a lot of factors. Ask your potential pediatrician their stance on vaccines, circumcisions, potty training, breastfeeding, complementary/alternative care, and other potentially touchy subjects. You'll want to find a doctor who is knowledgeable and is in alignment with your beliefs.

Going Home

Ask your doctors and nurses for any last tips before going home. Make sure your baby's first doctor's appointment is set, typically a few days to a week after going home.

Once your baby is in a super cute outfit and buckled into a car seat (rear-facing in the back seat of the car), it's time for the real adventure! Many parents say that the first drive with the baby is the scariest in their life. It can help to have one parent sit in the back with a pacifier, in case your baby wakes up and cries on the way home. Remember, it is unsafe and illegal to take your baby out of the car seat while driving. And a crying baby can be very distracting, so please stay safe!

Check page 87 for a list of essential baby items you will need when you get home. And make sure you have your copy of *The Baby Manual* with you!

Chapter 2

Basic Baby Care

These are the basic skills
every parent needs

How to Hold a Baby

There are three important things to consider when holding your baby, or allowing others to hold your baby:

1. **Support the neck.** Babies' heads are much larger (and heavier) in proportion to their body than adults' heads are. Babies lack the neck muscles to support their own neck, so it is very important that every time your baby is held, the neck is supported. The head should be in line with the body, not tilted forward or backward.

2. **Be aware of the fontanels (soft spots).** There is a large soft spot towards the front of your baby's crown (the anterior fontanel), and a small one at the back (the posterior fontanel). Sometimes the posterior fontanel closes during birth, and sometimes later, but should close before 2 months of age. The anterior fontanel should shrink over time, and close completely by 1 year of age. These soft spots lie between the bones of the skull, and they are places where your baby's brain is less protected from impact. It is ok to feel for the soft spots, but do not press too firmly on them.

3. **Do not let your baby fall.** Take extra care when lifting your baby or handing your baby to someone else to hold. Hold your baby close to your body for stability. Children who wish to hold the new baby should be seated on the couch with an adult supervising, like in the picture to the right. Also, never leave your baby alone on a changing table, bed, couch, or any other high surface. Babies can scoot and fall off of surfaces before they are able to roll over.

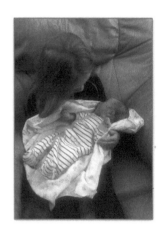

How to Change a Diaper

Newborn babies go through an average of 10-12 diapers per day. Make sure you are stocked up!

1. The first part is figuring out which is the front and which is the back of the diaper. The back of the diaper has tabs, which fold toward the front. Some disposable diapers have pictures in the front and/or a yellow stripe that turns green when it gets wet with urine.

2. Make sure the changing table is ready. There should be a blanket for baby to lie on, damp washcloths or baby wipes and a clean diaper. You may also want diaper cream, some toys or a mobile for distraction, and a pacifier on or near the changing table.

3. Place your baby on the changing table face up. Never leave your baby unattended on the table! If you need to look away, place one hand on your baby before turning your head.

4. Gain access to the soiled diaper by moving/removing clothing. Do not open the diaper yet.

5. Unfold the clean diaper, and place the back half under baby's bottom and the soiled diaper, like in the picture on the right.

6. Open the soiled diaper, and use any clean parts on the inside to gently wipe away any stool that might be stuck to baby. Then use a damp washcloth or baby wipe to clean the area. Be aware that opening the diaper and/or wiping may cause your baby to urinate or pass stool - stand to the side, out of the line of fire!

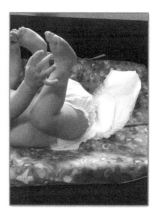

- For baby girls, always wipe front to back (from the vaginal opening toward the rectum) to avoid infection. If there is any stool on the labia, use your fingers to gently separate the labia and wipe the stool away. Only clean what you can see; do not clean inside the vagina. It is normal for newborn girls to have a white vaginal discharge, and sometimes blood (a "false period"), for the first week or two after birth. These are caused by maternal hormones and will go away.

- For circumcised boys, gently retract the penile skin away from the glans. The glans is the head of the penis, so you will be retracting toward the body, to make sure adhesions are not forming. Adhesions can cause a poor cosmetic outcome, and may even need to be removed surgically. It's best to prevent them! After retracting the skin, put a dime-sized amount of petroleum jelly on the wound, and a piece of gauze or a cotton cosmetic pad over it. Do this until it is healed, which should take 2-7 days. Once the circumcision is healed, just wipe the area normally.

- For uncircumcised (also called "intact") boys, there is no need to retract the foreskin and clean the glans. One way to remember this is "when intact, don't retract, only clean what can be seen." You can wipe your child normally, and during bath time clean the area with soap and water just as you clean the rest of the body. As your baby grows up, the foreskin will become retractile, and it will be possible to clean underneath it. This can happen anytime between age 2 and 18 years (it's a huge range), so just allow it to happen and don't try to forcibly retract the foreskin.

7. Apply diaper cream. Spread a fingertip- sized amount, thinly onto baby's bottom around the anus and in the leg creases. If your baby has a diaper rash, the cream should be applied over the entire rash. If the cream isn't making the rash go away, it may be infected, so call your doctor.

8. Roll up the soiled diaper from front to back, sliding your baby's bottom onto the new diaper as you do so. Fold the tabs on the back over the front to close the soiled diaper.

9. Close the new diaper by folding the front half up, and using the side tabs. When the umbilical cord is still attached, roll down the front before closing it with the tabs, so the diaper sits below the umbilical cord. Once the umbilical cord has fallen off, you can close the diaper normally without folding.

Umbilical Cord Care

Immediately after birth, your baby's umbilical cord will be clamped with a plastic clip. This will be removed in a few days, leaving behind the remaining umbilical cord. This cord is not attached to any major nerves, so touching it does not hurt the baby. The cord will turn yellow, brown, or black as it dries up.

Keep the cord clean and dry by washing your hands before touching it, folding down the front of the diaper below the cord, and dressing your baby in loose-fitting clothing that allows air flow around the cord. It is not necessary to disinfect the stump with alcohol or iodine, but you can clean it with alcohol if you notice blood or yellowish discharge.

Avoid getting the cord wet. You should wash your baby with a damp washcloth while the cord is still intact. After it falls off you can transition your baby to baths.

Call your doctor if you think the umbilical cord might be getting infected. Signs of infection are foul-smelling discharge and redness of the skin around the cord.

The cord should fall off around a week or two of age. As it is getting close to falling off, you might notice some blood and yellowish goo where the stump was attached, like in the picture to the right. This is totally normal; just wipe it away with a clean washcloth. If the area continues bleeding, you should call a doctor.

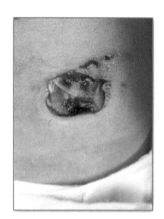

After the cord falls off, the belly button takes about another week to heal and to start looking like a regular belly button. If it takes longer than this, your baby may have an umbilical granuloma. Ask your doctor if you are concerned about this. The doctor may use a chemical called silver nitrate to cauterize the area; this is not painful for your baby.

How to Swaddle a Baby

Follow the steps below to swaddle:

1. Lay the blanket down on the bed (or other flat surface) in a diamond shape and fold down the top corner.

2. Place your baby on the blanket with the head resting on the folded corner.

3. Wrap one side of the diamond over your baby, and tuck the corner in tightly underneath.

4. Bring the bottom corner up as high as you can.

5. Wrap the other side around your baby tightly and tuck it in.

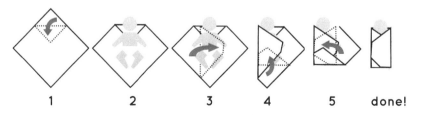

1   2   3   4   5   done!

Breathing Patterns

Newborns breathe episodically, meaning sometimes they will breathe fast for a few breaths, and slow for a few breaths. They might even pause for a few seconds, then continue breathing. It can be scary for new parents to watch, especially for NICU graduates. If your baby is at risk for apnea, your doctor may prescribe an apnea monitor. If your baby does not need an apnea monitor (most don't), then don't worry, it is probably a normal breathing pattern! If you are concerned, ask a doctor.

Crying - How Much is Too Much?

Babies use crying as their main form of communication. Most babies will cry a total of 2 hours per day. That works out to about 5 minutes out of every hour. Most newborns will sleep 2-3 hours at a time, so that really works out to about 10-15 minutes of crying each time baby wakes up. To help calm your baby, use a gentle rocking or swaying motion, or try singing or talking quietly to them.

To determine when crying is excessive (and to make a diagnosis of colic), we follow the rule of threes: 3 or more hours of crying per day, 3 or more days per week, for 3 weeks in a row. Colic peaks around 4-6 weeks of age.

Bathing Your Baby

Babies do not need to be bathed as often as adults. Your baby will likely be bathed by the hospital staff in the first few hours. During the first week, when the umbilical cord is still attached, you may clean your baby with a washcloth. Once the cord falls off, you may begin bathing in a baby bathtub. I recommend bathing babies 2-3 times per week with a mild, unscented soap and/or baby shampoo. After the bath, gently pat your baby dry with a soft towel. You may apply lotion after the bath, but realize that babies have sensitive skin and may get a rash from lotion.

Skin Care

Newborn babies' skin may peel for the first week or two. Imagine spending 9 months in a bath tub - your skin would peel too when you got out! Dry, peeling skin is normal and doesn't need any special treatments. It will go away on its own.

On the right, you can see a newborn's feet with normal dry, peeling skin. This amount of dryness and peeling doesn't need any lotion or ointment.

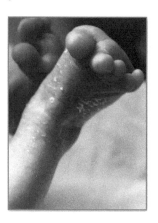

If the dry skin becomes severe and you start to see cracks, you can apply an emollient such as petroleum jelly, Aquaphor, or A&D ointment. Cracking and bleeding typically happens on the wrists and ankles if it's going to happen at all. It's best to apply emollients after a bath, because they will seal in the moisture from the bath water and help the cracked skin to heal faster.

Sneezes and Hiccups

You may have noticed that your baby sneezes and gets hiccups a lot. These are both totally normal!

Babies have tiny noses and they don't know how to blow their nose yet, so even the littlest bit of dry air or dust will cause their boogers to dry up and make them sneeze. Sneezing does not necessarily mean that your baby is sick or has allergies. Babies can catch colds, but allergies typically aren't diagnosed until age 3 years. If you think your baby might be getting a cold, you should call your pediatrician right away.

Hiccups are normal and don't bother your baby at all. Most moms will remember feeling their baby having hiccups while they were still on the inside. Hiccups in newborns are caused by the same process, a neurologic and respiratory system that are not fully mature yet. Your baby will outgrow the hiccups soon enough, so enjoy those cute little squeaks while you can!

Teething

Most babies will start getting teeth at 6 months of age, but it can happen any time in the first year. In fact, 1 in 2000 babies are born with teeth or get a tooth in the first month of life!

Signs of teething are increased fussiness, drooling, pink cheeks, low-grade fever, and chewing on hands or toys (as in the photo on the right). Babies can show signs of teething for months before actually getting teeth, so don't get too excited when you see these signs.

If your baby is in pain, you can let them chew on teething toys, use a topical medication such as Orajel, or give Tylenol. Check with your pediatrician about the best way to help your child with teething pain.

As soon as teeth erupt, you can and should brush them twice a day with a soft toothbrush. You can brush with plain water, or use a fluoride-free toothpaste that is designed for children too young to spit. And once your child has teeth, they should start seeing a pediatric dentist twice a year. The purpose is mostly to get your child used to being at the dentist, and decrease fear and anxiety around going to the dentist. Most dentist will only perform a small exam the first time, and can guide you on how to best brush your baby's teeth.

Chapter 3

Feeding Your Baby

*Newborn babies should only be fed
breastmilk and/or infant formula.*

How Much Should I Feed My Baby?

A newborn's stomach is about the size of a cherry, and can only hold about 1 tablespoon of milk at a time. By day 3 of life, your baby's stomach can hold about 1 ounce, and by 1 week of age your baby is able to eat up to 2 ounces at a time. By 1 month, your baby can eat up to 5 ounces at a time. This is about how big your baby's belly is:

1 day old   **2 days old**   **1 week old**   **1 month old**
5-7 ml   22-27 ml   45-60 ml   80-150 ml
1-1.4 tsp   0.75-1 oz   1.5-2 oz   2.5-5 oz

Newborns need to eat at least 8-10 times per day, which works out to about every 2-3 hours. The maximum length of time a newborn can go without eating is 4 hours. If your newborn baby sleeps for 4 hours straight, you need to wake your baby to eat.

Many newborns will "cluster feed," meaning they may eat several times in a row, then go a few hours before their next feed. This is totally normal! At the beginning, cluster feeding tends to happen during the wee hours of the morning. That's because prolactin, the hormone that makes women produce milk, naturally peaks in the early morning hours. Don't worry, the cluster feeding during the wee hours only lasts a few weeks. Soon your baby will learn the night-day difference and will start to eat more during the daytime and less at night.

Both breast milk and formula contain all of the carbohydrates, protein, fat, vitamins, minerals, and water that your baby needs for the first 4-6 months of life. After 4-6 months of age, you can begin to supplement with baby foods and water.

Breastfeeding

The American Academy of Pediatrics recommends exclusive breastfeeding for the first 6 months of life, with addition of baby food and supplemental water until age 1 year or later. The decision of when to stop breastfeeding rests between the mom and baby.

Make sure you take the following supplements the entire time you are breastfeeding:

- A prenatal vitamin that contains iron and folic acid
- Omega-3 fatty acids (200-300mg per day)
- Calcium (1000mg per day)
- Vitamin D (5,000-6,400 IU per day)

Benefits of Breastfeeding

1. Emotional benefits

   • Studies show that breastfeeding promotes a strong bong between mother and child.

   • When a baby sucks on a breast, it causes a release of oxytocin and beta endorphins in the brain. Oxytocin is a hormone that makes you feel good and form emotional attachments, and beta endorphins are hormones that make you feel happy and are natural painkillers.

2. Health benefits for mom

   • Breastfeeding shortly after delivery will decrease the amount of postpartum blood loss, as it helps your uterus return to its original size.

   • It can help you lose your baby weight faster, since it burns an additional 500 calories per day.

   • Mothers who breastfeed have a 28% decreased risk of breast cancer and ovarian cancer.

   • There is a 20% decreased risk of rheumatoid arthritis.

   • There is a decreased risk of postpartum depression.

   • Breastfeeding may stop your period and make it harder to get pregnant right away, although it is not a reliable birth control method.

3. Health benefits for baby

   • Breastfed babies have healthier eating habits later in life, and a decreased risk of developing obesity later in life. This is thought to be because they learn to self-regulate from the start, rather than being driven by how much is in the bottle. They also have a 40% decreased risk of type 2 diabetes as adults.

   • Breastmilk contains immunoglobulins, which are the proteins produced in the bloodstream in response to infection. This gives your baby passive immunity to fight off common germs. There is an overall 72-74% reduction in respiratory infections, 23-63% reduction in ear infections, and 64% reduction in gastrointestinal illness (diarrhea and vomiting) in breastfed vs. bottle-fed babies.

- There is a 58-77% decreased risk of necrotizing enterocolitis, a rare condition in preemies where parts of the intestines stop working and need to be removed.

- Breastfed babies have a 36% decreased risk of Sudden Infant Death Syndrome (SIDS).

- Babies of allergy-prone parents who exclusively breastfeed for 3-4 months have a 42% decreased risk of allergies, eczema, and asthma.

- There is a decreased risk of autoimmune disease. Breastfed babies have a 52% reduction in celiac disease (allergy to wheat gluten), 31% reduction in inflammatory bowel disease (Crohn's disease and ulcerative colitis), and a 30% reduction in type 1 diabetes (the kind that children get).

4. Added benefits that nobody really talks about

- Your baby's poo won't smell bad if you breastfeed exclusively.

- There is always the perfect amount. Each time you feed, your body responds to the demands of your baby, and produces as much as your baby needs.

- There is always food on hand for your baby, without having to carry extra bottles/formula. And it's always warm enough.

- The amounts of carbohydrates, fat, and proteins in your breastmilk change over time to meet your baby's needs, so your 1-month-old is getting different milk than they will get at 6 months of age.

- It's free. And formula is expensive.

Drawbacks to Breastfeeding

1. It can be difficult, and does not come naturally to most mothers. Take a breastfeeding class or find a Lactation Specialist to help you learn how to breastfeed. Give yourself and your baby at least 2 weeks to learn to breastfeed well!

2. It can be painful for the first week or two. Dry, cracked, and sore nipples are a common occurrence in the first 2 weeks. The skin on your nipples is similar to that on your lips, and think how your lips get chapped if you lick them too much. Your nipples are not used being sucked on 12 times a day, and they are bound to get chapped unless you aggressively moisturize them! Lanolin, coconut oil, olive oil, and petroleum jelly are all safe to rub on your nipples (i.e. you don't have to wipe them off before your baby eats) and may help. They are like lip balm for your nipples. I suggest putting on a thick layer after each time your baby breastfeeds, then using a disposable breast pad to protect your clothing. Even without dryness and cracking, you are bound to get sore. Ibuprofen is safe to take while breastfeeding and can help with the pain.

3. It can be inconvenient to find a time or place to breastfeed, though this is less of a problem nowadays as breastfeeding awareness spreads.

4. You can develop mastitis at any time if a milk duct stays full for too long. Mastitis is a painful condition, characterized by redness, swelling, pain, and fever, and often requires antibiotics. Massaging your breasts and feeling for lumps or swollen areas while feeding your baby or pumping can help prevent mastitis.

5. Certain infections and medications can prevent you from breastfeeding. Some diseases can pass through breast milk (tuberculosis, human T-cell lymphotrophic virus, brucellosis, chicken pox, HIV) or through contact (herpes or shingles on the breast). Check with your doctor if you take any medications. Most medications that you can't take during pregnancy are ok to take when you are breastfeeding. The same goes for vaccines (such as MMR and chicken pox). This is because when you are pregnant, it is easy for substances in your bloodstream to pass through the placenta and into your baby's bloodstream. It is much harder for substances to pass into breast milk.

Giving Bottles of Breastmilk

Breastmilk can be expressed with a pump and given to your baby later. This is a great way for breastfeeding moms to let other family members feed and bond with the baby. It's also helpful for mothers who have a schedule that does not allow for frequent-enough breastfeeding.

Breastmilk will last different amounts of time at different temperatures. The rule of six is easy to remember. You can refer to the diagram to the right if you forget. The rule is:

- Breastmilk lasts for 6 months in the freezer, 6 days in the fridge, and 6 hours at room temperature.

- The exception: breastmilk that has been moved out of the freezer to thaw in the fridge will only keep for 1 day. That's because the protective antibodies in human milk are inactivated by freezing.

Tips on Pumping

There are many types of breast pumps available - choose one that works for you! Things to take into consideration:

- Is it a manual or electric pump? Electric pumps tend to be faster and also cost more, and are great if you plan on primarily feeding your baby bottles of breast milk (for example, if you are going back to work full time, if your baby is in the NICU, or you are unable to physically breastfeed for another reason). Manual pumps are great for the occasional bottle of breastmilk.

- Can you adjust the amount of suction? You need the right amount of suction, as too little can be ineffective at pumping milk out, and too much can be painful.

- Is it portable? Some electric pumps plug into a wall and can be large and difficult to transport to work. Battery-operated pumps are more portable, but can go through batteries quickly, so you will need to carry backups. Manual pumps tend to be easiest to transport, but don't allow for handsfree pumping.

- Single or double?   It depends whether you want to pump from one side at a time, or both at the same time. Double pumps are easiest to use with a pumping bra - you can either buy a pumping bra, or use an old sports bra and cut slits in it to hold the pump in place. It needs to fit snugly to hold the pump in place.

How to get the most out of pumping:

- Pump early in the morning, when your prolactin level is naturally at its peak.

- Pump on one side while your baby is latched on the other side, or pump within 15 minutes of feeding your baby. The natural hormones released during breastfeeding will increase your supply. If you are unable to breastfeed your baby, snuggling with your baby or looking at a photo can have a similar effect on milk production.

- Stay hydrated! You need to drink extra water to produce enough milk; at least 8 glasses of water per day.

- You can try herbal teas, lactation cookies, and other dietary supplements to keep your supply up.   Many of these remedies are anecdotal (not studied in clinical trials) but are also typically harmless to try, so why not?

- Remember, you must continue your prenatal vitamin, omega-3 fatty acids, calcium, and vitamin D supplements the entire time you are pumping!

Choosing the Right Baby Formula

There are many types of formula on the market, and many brands as well. I recommend choosing a formula and sticking with it for a few weeks before deciding that your baby doesn't tolerate it. Babies need several days, sometimes even 2-3 weeks, to get used to a new formula.   Beware of "formula roulette," where colicky babies are started on a new formula every few days, and never really improve. In fact, changing formulas too often can worsen colic, gas, and spit-ups. If you are thinking of starting a new formula, talk with your pediatrician about it first. Selecting a new formula at random can make your baby worse.

These are the main types of formula:

- Regular cow's-milk-based formula. This type of formula is designed to mimic human milk. Newborn formula is meant to be given during the first month of life, and then infant formula is used after that (from 1-11 months). This is the type of formula that most babies will eat. Store brands and generics are equal in terms of nutrition and quality, so choose a brand that best fits your budget.

- Preemie formula. The last month inside the womb is when babies store the majority of their iron and calcium, and build up their baby fat. This means that babies who are born prematurely need more calcium, iron, and calories than babies born at term. Preemie formula is designed to meet these needs.

- Soy formula. The main medical reason to use soy formula is in a rare genetic condition called galactosemia. Some doctors will prescribe soy formula after a baby has diarrhea, because the viruses that cause diarrhea can cause a temporary lactose intolerance. One personal reason to use soy formula is for a family that is vegan. Soy formulas are an acceptable (and slightly more expensive) alternative to cow's-milk-based formulas. Soy formula should NOT be given to babies with milk protein allergy - you must talk to your doctor if you think you child has an allergy or intolerance to cow's milk.

- Anti-reflux formula. For babies with significant reflux, there are formulas containing rice starch that thicken when they mix with stomach acid. This helps keep the formula in your baby's belly. Your doctor might prescribe this type of formula if your baby has reflux.

- Sensitive formula. For children with gas and spit-ups, these formulas have more simple sugars that are easier to digest and will help soothe upset tummies.

- Hydrolyzed formulas. These formulas smell (and taste) terrible and are extremely expensive, but are sometimes the only option for babies with very strict dietary needs due to an underlying medical condition. Hydrolyzed formulas have carbohydrates, fats, and/or proteins that have been broken down (pre-digested) into their building blocks for easier digestion. Some formulas are more extensively hydrolyzed than others. Some babies have an allergy to the proteins in regular and soy formula, so doctors prescribe hydrolyzed formula to these babies.

How to Prepare Formula

It is ok to mix up one day's worth of formula at a time, and keep it in the refrigerator. Just heat it up before giving it to your baby. You should not keep prepared formula in the fridge for more than a day, because it will spoil.

Newborns typically eat 2-3 ounces of formula every 2-3 hours, or 24 ounces per day. As your baby grows, you will notice your baby consuming more formula. You should always have a little bit of formula left in the bottle after feeding your baby; if your baby finishes off a bottle, it means you need to make an extra ounce the next time. Always throw away any extra formula that is left in the bottle.

Some formula is sold ready-to-feed; it is extremely convenient, but also expensive, heavy to transport, and it takes up a lot of space in the pantry. So most parents will quickly switch to powdered formula. The powdered formula should be exactly the same as the ready-to-feed.

To make powdered formula, you should follow the instructions on the package exactly. Never make formula that is more concentrated or diluted than the instructions, because your baby could get very sick.

A Few Notes on Bottle Feeding

Whether you are giving your baby formula or breastmilk in a bottle, you should remember these things.

- Before giving a bottle to your baby, it should be warmed up to body temperature. The best is to place the bottle in a bowl of hot water and swirl it around. You should not boil or microwave breast milk or formula. You can check the temperature by putting a few drops of milk on the inside of your wrist; it should not feel hot or cold, but the same temperature as your skin.

- Do not push the bottle into your baby's mouth. Instead, gently brush the nipple near the corner of your baby's mouth, and let your baby latch on to the bottle.

- Keep the bottle tilted so the nipple is always full of liquid, so your baby doesn't swallow too much air while eating. This will help avoid reflux, gas, and colic.

- Always hold onto the bottle the entire time you are feeding your baby. Never prop the bottle on pillows, or allow a newborn to hold the bottle - your baby could choke. If a sibling is feeding the baby, make sure they are supervised the entire time. Never put a baby to bed with a bottle.

- Burp your baby after each ounce of milk.

- Anything left in the bottle needs to be thrown away. Do not refrigerate or re-freeze the extra milk; it's not safe.

How to Tell when Your Baby is Done Eating

If your baby starts falling asleep, sucks more slowly, or turns away from the breast/bottle, the meal is probably over. But sometimes babies will consume an entire bottle/breast and continue to root around and fuss. Babies love to suck even after they finish eating. This is because the stomach takes several minutes to send a signal to the brain saying that it is full. A pacifier can help soothe your baby while the full feeling sinks in.

If you over-feed babies, they end up spitting up and/or getting diarrhea. If this happens, be sure to stop often and burp your baby in the middle of feeding. Then try giving a pacifier.

If your baby still seems hungry after a feeding (is awake, rooting, or fussing), and you've tried giving a pacifier and waiting it out, you may need to feed your baby again. Babies sometimes "cluster feed" - they may want several meals in a row, a few times per day. This is normal - there is no need to force your baby to wait 2-3 hours between feedings.

When can I Start Solids?

Most babies will be ready to start solids (pureed foods) at 4-6 months of age. Check with your pediatrician at the 4-month visit to see if your baby is ready. Signs of readiness include:

- Ability to sit with support - your baby should have good head control, meaning holding the head straight up, while sitting in a lap or in a high chair (as in the picture on the right).

- Loss of the extrusion reflex - the extrusion reflex means sticking out the tongue when something is brought to the mouth. You can test this with an empty baby spoon - if your baby sucks on the spoon rather than sticking out the tongue, your baby is ready to be fed solids.

- Bringing hands and objects into the mouth

How to Introduce Solids

I recommend starting with rice cereal, since it is unlikely to cause food allergies. You can mix dry rice cereal with breast milk or formula, until it has a consistency somewhere between applesauce and mashed potatoes. If the cereal runs down your baby's face, it is too thin, so add more dry cereal. If your baby gags while eating, it is too thick, so add more breast milk or formula. If your baby spits out the cereal or seems to choke, it means your baby is not quite ready for solids, so wait a week and then try again.

Once your baby tolerates rice cereal, you can start with pureed foods. I recommend starting with vegetables, one at a time, and start with the yucky vegetables first. It's up to you to decide which vegetables are the yucky ones. Since your baby has never tasted anything like this before, each food should seem delicious as it's discovered.

One suggestion is to start with peas, broccoli, and squash. Then move on to the sweeter vegetables such as carrots and sweet potatoes. After that, start fruits such as banana, apple, and pear. Once your baby is eating the sweet foods, the vegetables won't taste as good, and you may find that your baby spits the food out or makes a yucky face. So start with the yucky ones first, while they are still new and delicious!

You can feed your baby 1-2oz of solid foods once a day to start, and gradually increase up to 3-5x per day. There's a saying that "food before one is just for fun," meaning the solid foods that your baby eats in the first year of life are meant to teach your baby eating and swallowing skills, and are not necessarily the mainstay of nutrition. Your baby's diet should consist mainly of breast milk or formula until 1 year of age. After 1 year of age, your baby should transition to eating 3 meals per day, with snacks in between, water for hydration, and breast milk, formula, or cow's milk to supplement.

When your baby is eating solids/purees, you should start giving your baby water. I recommend about 1oz of water for every 2oz of baby food or rice cereal. If your baby is constipated, you can increase the water.

Food Allergies

Some children are more likely than others to develop food allergies. These include children with a family member who has any allergies (to foods, medications, or even hay fever), asthma, and/or eczema. Also babies who have cradle cap and eczema are more likely to develop food allergies.

Food allergies in children usually appear in the form of a rash, and the rash may appear right away, or it may appear after eating a new food for a few days. So the general recommendation is to start only one new food at a time, for 3 days, before starting another new food. Imagine, if you gave your baby 3 new foods at once and your baby got a rash, you wouldn't know which of the foods caused it and you'd have to cut out all 3 from your baby's diet. Adding one food at a time allows you to know which food, if any, your baby is allergic to.

The top 8 foods that cause allergies in children are: peanuts, tree nuts, fish, shellfish, dairy, wheat, egg, and soy. Pay special attention when starting these foods, but keep in mind that any food can cause an allergy.

If you have a family member with an allergy, and your baby has severe eczema, your baby is considered to be at high risk for a peanut allergy. The recent research shows that in these babies, it's best to introduce peanut protein early. You can put a tiny dab of peanut butter on your finger for your baby to suck off, or mix a pea-sized amount of peanut butter with baby cereal or pureed fruit. If you notice a rash after trying peanuts, call your doctor for advice on how to proceed.

Baby-Led Weaning

The idea of baby-led weaning is that you hand solid foods to your baby (such as slices of fruits and vegetables) and allow your baby to suck on these foods and eventually eat them, without the parent putting the food into the baby's mouth. Baby-led weaning skips purees and goes straight to solid foods.

Baby-led weaning is not currently supported by the American Academy of Pediatrics, because it carries a high risk of choking. Check with your doctor if you are considering baby-led weaning.

Nipple Confusion

Some parents fear that giving a pacifier or a bottle to a breastfeeding baby will cause nipple confusion, meaning the baby will become confused about which shape of nipple to suck on, and they worry that breastfeeding will fail. This is not true. What does happen though, is babies prefer to drink milk from whatever source has the highest flow, and sometimes babies who are offered a bottle will refuse to breastfeed.

Using a bottle with a standard-flow nipple will allow the milk to flow faster than it does out of the breast. Once a baby realizes how easy it is to get milk out of a bottle with minimal sucking, it is hard to get that baby to work harder again by breastfeeding. One way to prevent this from happening is to use slow-flow or preemie nipples on bottles for your newborn. The flow on those nipples is similar to that of human nipples.

Human milk and formula do taste different, and you may find that your baby prefers the taste of one over the other. This is not nipple confusion either.

Pacifiers do not cause nipple confusion, and can be soothing for your baby and reduce the incidence of SIDS. Pacifiers come in many shapes and sizes, and some babies will prefer one shape over another. You can experiment with various pacifiers to find one your baby likes. Some babies will prefer to suck on their thumb or fingers, and that is ok too. Sucking a thumb or finger won't cause nipple confusion.

Chapter 4

Pooping and Peeing

Do you know what normal newborn poop and pee look like, and how often they should go? Read on to find out!

Normal Poop (Stool)

Newborns will stool approximately once each time they eat, or about 8-12 times per day. Formula-fed babies will typically have smelly stools, while breastfed babies typically have stools that do not smell very much at all.

The first type of stool your newborn will have is called meconium. It is dark green in color, and a thick, sticky consistency (a little thicker than jelly). Some babies will pass meconium in utero; this is more common in babies who are born after their due date. Most babies will start having meconium stools in the first 48 hours of life. They typically last for a day or two, before turning into soft, yellow-green transitional stool.

During the first few weeks, your baby's stool should become mustard-yellow with light seedy pieces in it. The consistency is thin but not liquid, similar to that of mustard.

Over the first few months, the yellow seedy stool will gradually become slightly firmer, more uniform in consistency, and more brownish in color. For the first 4-6 months (before baby eats solid foods), each stool should be about the consistency of toothpaste.

These colors are all normal for stool, and the color usually changes in this order:

Diarrhea

Since normal newborn and infant stools are very soft in nature, it can be difficult to tell if your baby has diarrhea. But it is very important to know what diarrhea in infants looks like, because they can quickly become severely dehydrated from diarrhea. If you think your baby has diarrhea, you should consult with a doctor immediately. Typical signs of diarrhea in infants are:

- Stool that is so watery that it soaks into the diaper

- A marked increase in the number of stools beyond what your baby normally has, for example several times per hour instead of once every 2-3 hours

- Stools that are so large in volume that they cause a "blowout" and leak outside the diaper - this may happen once in a while, but should not happen for more than 2 diapers in a row

- Rumbly stomach noises and copious gas while stooling

- A very foul smell to the stool that was not there previously, typically accompanied by a change in color and consistency

- Fever (not always present)

- Blood in stool (not always present)

Constipation

Around 4-6 weeks of life, your baby will stop stooling every 2-3 hours. This is the age when children start to experience **discoordinate stooling** - they are learning how to control the anal sphincter, and they will often squeeze the sphincter and the abdominal muscles at the same time, causing a great buildup of pressure without allowing the stool to pass. These babies will grunt, turn red in the face, and even cry as they squeeze all of their muscles tightly. At this time, most parents believe their child is constipated. The way to tell that this is discoordinate stooling and not constipation is that when the stool finally does pass, it is nice and soft.

Only about 3% of infants get truly constipated. Signs of constipation in infancy are:

- Firm stools that are the consistency of rocks or pellets

- Pain during bowel movement (not always apparent)

- Rectal bleeding (not always present)

Treatment of constipation in infants is a little different than in older children. Options include:

- Prune juice, 1-2 ounces per day. This is a strong laxative in infants and should be thought of as a medication and not a fruit juice. Infants can have one-half to one ounce in a bottle before a feeding in the morning, and again at night if needed. Use prune juice carefully, as it may cause diarrhea.

- Sometimes changing formula can cause constipation, so reverting to the original formula, or trying one that is targeted toward constipation can help.

- Once your baby is eating rice cereal and other solids, it's important to make sure your baby has enough fluid intake. I typically recommend an ounce of water for each serving of cereal or baby food.

Normal Urine

During the first few days of life, your newborn may only void a handful of times. But after the first few days, it is normal for a newborn to void 8-12 times per day, or every 2-3 hours. They should void about every time they eat. It is sometimes hard to gage how much urine is being passed, since it soaks into the diaper, and often gets obscured by stool. Most disposable diapers have a yellow stripe that turns blue when it reacts to urine. The stripe won't change if it's wet from only stool.

The color of newborn urine is variable, but should be similar to the color of adult urine. Some babies will pass rust-colored urine or crystals into their diaper during the first few days. This is normal and goes away on its own. The urine progressively lightens, until it reaches the normal adult color by 1 week of age. Here are some normal colors of urine:

Decreased Urination

Decreased urination can indicate that your baby is dehydrated. This is more common in warm weather or if your baby has a fever. If your baby pees less than 6 times in 24 hours, you should call your doctor.

Blood in the Diaper

Some newborn females have pseudomenses, or a "false period." This typically occurs when baby girls are about 5-10 days old, and is a normal process caused by withdrawal of maternal hormones. It shouldn't last more than a few days, and you will notice that there is blood in the diaper that is separate from the urine or the stool. You might even see blood on or around the labia during diaper changes. Remember, this is not painful or dangerous. It is a normal process and will go away in a few days.

Blood in the urine or stool, on the other hand, is never normal. If your baby has bloody urine (and is more than a few days old so you know it's not the normal rust-colored urine), it could be a sign of kidney problems. Blood in the stool can be from an infection or food allergy. You need to call a doctor immediately when there is blood in the urine or stool. It helps to bring the bloody diaper with you.

As your baby gets older and tries new food, remember that some foods mimic blood in the diaper (beets, tomatoes, and watermelon are typical culprits). If you aren't sure, bring the diaper to the doctor's office and ask! They can do a quick test for blood.

Potty Training and Elimination Communication

Did you know, you can start potty training your baby as early as birth? This method is sometimes called "diaper free" but is more accurately termed "elimination communication" or EC, as it involves reading your baby's cues and giving your baby cues when it is time to potty.

Babies don't want to sit in their own waste. That is why babies cry when they have a wet or soiled diaper. Starting potty training early can reduce discomfort in your baby, decrease the likelihood of diaper rash, help avoid a major struggle in toddlerhood, and cut back on the number of diapers you'll go through. I recommend starting around 1-2 months of age, or as soon as the number of poops decreases from every diaper change to a few per day.

To start, you'll need to decide what phrase and/or hand signal you will use to let your child know it's time to potty. Even something simple like, "let's go potty" works! If you use the same phrase every time, your child will quickly learn what it means.

To do EC, you will hold your baby over a sink or hold them on a potty chair or adapter for the potty. You can see a baby on a potty adapter on the right. Remember, never leave your baby alone on the potty! You can help inspire your baby to pee by making a "psssss" sound or running water from the tap, and to poop by making a grunting or straining sound.

An easy way to start with potty training or elimination communication is with the easy catches. Here are a few:

- If your baby pees every time you change the diaper, you are in luck! This is a really easy catch. Loosen the diaper, carry your baby to the bathroom with the diaper held against their body, and take the diaper off and put them on the potty or over the sink as soon as you take the diaper off.

- Babies need to potty after eating because of the gastro-colic reflex, which is when the tummy fills and the intestines move.

- When your baby wakes up in the morning or after a nap, this is another natural and easy time to take them to potty.

- If you see your baby starting to poop (by staring off into space for a moment, then grunting and pushing) you can say "wait!" and then use the potty phrase, and immediately take them to potty. You might miss the first few, but your baby will learn quickly that "wait" means they are about to get to go in the potty and they will hold it if possible. A baby cannot and will not wait to the point that they are in pain, so don't worry that you are causing your child to be uncomfortable. If your baby needs to go, they will, whether or not they are in a diaper.

Some signs that your baby may need to potty are wiggling, fussing, or crying, especially if they are well-rested and have just eaten. Watch your baby for signs, as every baby is different.

Potty training from birth can take several months, and works best when there is consistency among all caregivers. So this might not be an option for children going into daycare early, or for families who don't have time to devote to watching their baby's cues. And there's no problem with the traditional American method of waiting until 2-4 years to potty train your child. Elimination communication is just one of many options, and one that many parents have not heard of in the US. It's much more common in other countries.

For more information you can search online for websites and videos about elimination communication, potty training from birth, or the diaper free method.

Chapter 5

Helping Your Baby Sleep at Night

Here are some tips to help you and baby get more rest.

Understand Baby Sleep Patterns

Newborns sleep up to 18 hours per day, in 2-3 hour increments. It's not safe to allow your baby to sleep more than 4 hours at a time during the first month. If your baby sleeps for more than 4 hours, you must wake your baby up to eat. The frequent nighttime wakings will disrupt both parents' schedules, but fear not! This phase will pass. Once your baby has surpassed birth weight and is gaining steadily, you can allow your baby to sleep more than 4 hours at a time. Check with your pediatrician to see whether it is ok to let your baby sleep more than 4 hours.

Around 4-6 weeks, your baby will start to sleep slightly more at night, and slightly less during the day. Your baby will still wake up at least 1-3 times during the night to eat and be changed.

By 6 months, your baby may able to sleep for long periods of time (8-12 hours), but many babies will still wake up at least once per night. Establishing good sleep hygiene will help your baby sleep more soundly. But remember, even if you do all the "right" things, your baby may still wake up several times at night. This is not a reflection on you as a parent, it is simply your baby's sleep pattern.

Notice Signs that Your Baby is Tired

Infants will let you know when they are getting ready to fall asleep. Drooping eyelids, rubbing the eyes, yawning, and fussing can all be signs that your baby needs to rest. Start getting your baby into bed when you see these signs. You should not allow your baby to fall asleep in your arms or wait until your baby is overtired - these can make it harder for your baby to sleep well.

Allow Your Baby to Fall Asleep Without Help

Always put your baby to bed drowsy and not asleep, so your baby can learn to fall asleep without relying on your help. Some parents prefer to allow their baby to fall asleep in their arms, while being rocked, while eating, or with a parent sitting next to them. These parents can expect to get up several times during the night to perform the same routine, even when their child is much older.

Allow a Reasonable Amount of Crying

Most babies will seem to wake up a little more when you first lie them down, and many will cry to be picked up again. This may be a sign that your baby is overtired. It is alright to allow your baby to cry for a few minutes before falling asleep. You should not allow your child to cry to the point of gasping or vomiting, but neither should you pick them up at the first peep. It is up to you as a parent to determine what a reasonable amount of crying is; generally 5-20 minutes is ok.

This is not the same as allowing your baby to "cry it out," which is crying to the point that they become exhausted and fall asleep. I do not recommend the "crying it out" method - it is not good for your baby.

Help Your Infant Distinguish Day from Night

When your baby wakes from napping during the day, demonstrate that it is a good time to be awake by playing, talking, laughing, singing, and otherwise interacting positively with your baby. When your baby awakes at night, keep the interaction and stimulation to a minimum. Keep the lights dim and speak in a quiet voice. Your baby will soon learn that nighttime is for sleeping, and daytime is for playing. By teaching the night/day difference to your newborn, your child will sleep better at night as a toddler and onward.

Swaddle Your Baby for the First Month

Newborns love to be swaddled tightly! Many people think that a baby floats around inside the womb like an astronaut on a spacewalk. This is not true at all! The womb is a very tight space, and just barely fits a baby inside. Your baby is used to being curled up tightly in the fetal position and held that way by the strong walls of the uterus. Once your baby is born, the lack of support in all directions is unsettling.

Your newborn baby's muscles are not strong enough to stay curled up tightly, so it's up to you to swaddle your baby with a blanket and make sure the arms and legs are not able to flail around. See page 11 for instructions on how to swaddle.

Once your baby is strong enough to bust out of the swaddled blanket, it's ok to stop swaddling. But if you find that your baby tends to break free from the swaddle and then wake up from arms flailing around, your baby may benefit from using a velcro swaddle blanket, a sleep suit, or a sleep sack.

When to Wake your Baby

Newborns need to eat every 2-4 hours throughout the day. For the first two months of life, if your baby has been asleep for 4 hours, it is time to wake your baby for a feeding. By 2 months of age your baby should be gaining weight steadily, and should be able to wake up when hungry. Ask your pediatrician if you are not sure whether it is ok to allow your baby to sleep more than 4 hours without waking up to eat.

Back to Sleep and SIDS

The current recommendation from the AAP is "Back to Sleep," which means babies should sleep flat on their backs (i.e. face up) in a crib/bassinet with nothing else in the crib except a light blanket. That means no pillow, no toys, no stuffed animals, and no extra blankets. This is to help reduce the risk of sudden infant death syndrome (SIDS). You can see an example in the photo to the right.

Another way to reduce the risk of SIDS is the use of a pacifier at bedtime, so it is ok to let your newborn fall asleep with a pacifier. The biggest risk factor for SIDS is parents smoking in the house, so this is a good time to stop smoking, or at the very least to step outside to smoke, then wash your hands with soap and water and change your clothing before interacting with your baby.

Around 4-6 months of age, there may be times that you put your baby to sleep face up, and return to find your baby has turned over while sleeping. This is normal and not dangerous if your baby is the one turning over. You should continue to place your baby face up to fall asleep at night, but if your baby rolls over there is no need to turn your baby back in the middle of the night.

Divide and Conquer for More Sleep

It can be a great relief for parents to split the nighttime responsibilities of feeding and changing your baby. Two popular options are splitting each night and alternating every other night. When splitting each night, one parent could take the 10pm-2am shift, and the other could take 2am-6am. When alternating nights, the parent who will be feeding and diapering that night can sleep in the baby's room, so the other parent can have a full night's sleep. Breastfeeding moms can pump during the day and sleep through the night, or pump during the night while the other parent gives bottles of breast milk.

I do not recommend having one parent feed and the other change diapers at night, because both parents will lose sleep that way. It is much better to have one parent do both the feeding and changing, either for half the night or every other night, so the other can have uninterrupted sleep.

Remember, both parents are exhausted and sleep deprived, so have compassion for your spouse. The first 3-6 months are the hardest, but it gets better! Hang in there. If at all possible, have a friend or family member come over to hold the baby so you can take a nap during the day. There is really no such thing as "sleep while the baby sleeps," but having someone to tend to the baby for an hour or two during the day can allow you the time to catch up on missed sleep.

Tips to Help You Sleep Better:

1. Keep your bedroom dark and quiet. Your baby will make many noises during the night (including cooing, snoring, and crib creaking), so a white noise machine can help if you are a light sleeper.

2. Avoid caffeine and alcohol. These will diminish the quality of the sleep that you get, and make you feel more tired overall. Drink plenty of water instead.

3. Minimize your screen time. You might think you are resting, but nothing can replace actual sleep, and the blue light from TVs, computers, phones, and tablets will decrease sleep quality by making it more difficult for your body to reach a deep sleep.

4. Eat healthy power snacks at night. A small serving of yogurt, fruit, or nuts will help you to have more energy when you wake up in the morning. Avoid eating large/heavy meals late at night, as these may make it harder for you to fall asleep.

5. Know that your baby's cry will wake you quicker than any alarm clock could. Go to sleep assured that you will be

woken up if your baby needs something (unless your newborn is sleeping more than 4 hours, in which case you do need to set an alarm).

6. Avoid co-sleeping with the baby. Parents who co-sleep have poorer sleep quality and sleep fewer hours than those whose babies sleep in their own crib or bassinet. Plus co-sleeping is a risk factor for SIDS.

Chapter 6

How Vaccines Work

The purpose of vaccines is to trigger an immune response faster and with less harm than the original disease.

Risk vs. Benefit

All vaccines that are available in the US have been proven to safely fight disease. And just like any medication, any vaccine can have side-effects. It is up to you to decide whether the risk of vaccination outweighs the benefit. The decision to vaccinate should be based on factual information and not on fear - either fear of the disease or fear of the vaccine itself. Speak to your doctor or another trusted healthcare professional if you are unsure about vaccinating. For the most current vaccine information and recommendations, the CDC publishes an updated vaccination schedule annually on their website, www.cdc.gov/vaccines.

How do Vaccines Work?

Your body's immune system is a lot like a microscopic team of superheroes, made up of white blood cells, antibodies, the complement system, and a few others. These superheroes fight villains such as bacteria, viruses, and other pathogens. If they cannot fight them fast enough, the villains will multiply and cause symptoms of disease. Vaccines will give your superhero team a picture of what the villains look like, so they can recognize them as soon as they enter the body, and fight them off quicker and easier.

There are 3 main types of vaccines:

- Inactivated (killed pathogens)
- Live attenuated (weakened pathogens)
- Toxoid (a piece of what's inside the pathogen)

Inactivated vaccines are the most common type. The bacteria or viruses in the vaccine are killed, so your immune system can safely learn to recognize the pathogen that it is trying to fight off. These vaccines do not have the potential to cause actual disease. What they do is cause the immune system superheroes to practice fighting the villains, kind of like practicing on dummies, which may cause mild signs of illness - fever, sore muscles, crankiness, or other symptoms. Some examples of inactivated vaccines are IPV (polio), HPV (human papillomavirus), HiB (*Haemophilus influenzae B*), pneumococcus (*Streptococcus pneumoniae*), meningococcus (*Neisseria meningitidis*), and Hepatitis A and B vaccines.

Live attenuated vaccines are the next most common. These are made from bacteria or viruses that have been exposed to chemicals that make them weaker than the natural or "wild type" bacteria or virus. Since these pathogens are not killed completely, your superheroes aren't just practicing on dummies, they are actually fighting the weakened villains. So it is possible to have symptoms that mimic the disease, but less severe. Some people with weakened immune systems may not be able to fight them off, and can get the actual disease. People taking steroid medications or immune suppressants, or who have HIV or other immune deficiencies should consult a doctor about whether it is safe to receive these vaccines. Some examples of live attenuated vaccines are the MMR (measles, mumps, and rubella), *Varicella zoster* (chickenpox), and rotavirus vaccines.

Toxoid vaccines are made from just part of the pathogen, and protect against the kinds of bacteria that cause symptoms after the toxins inside them are released. These toxin-carrying bacteria are like villains carrying around a bottle of poison, and the toxoid vaccine gives the superheroes the poison to sample and build up resistance to it. An example of a toxoid vaccine is the DTaP (diphtheria, tetanus, and acellular pertussis).

Top Concerns about Vaccines

Many parents have concerns about vaccinating their children. It only takes one serious reaction to call into question the safety of vaccines. And it has been so long since the vaccine-preventable diseases have run rampant that we in the United States don't fully understand the scope of what is being prevented. Here are some of the top concerns that I have heard from parents, and the truth behind them.

- Aluminum. There is aluminum in vaccines, but the amount is far less than babies get from other sources. The total amount of aluminum that babies get from vaccines in the first 6 months is 4.4mg. Breastfed babies consume 7mg, formula-fed babies consume 38mg, and babies on soy formula consume 114mg of aluminum in the first 6 months of life. Eating aluminum vs. having it injected in a vaccine looks the same to the body, so the tiny amount of aluminum in vaccines will not harm your baby.

- Antigens. An antigen is any microscopic substance that has the possibility to elicit an immune response. Babies are exposed to over a trillion antigens in the first year that naturally occur in the environment. The entire vaccine series that children receive today contains just over 150 antigens. A young baby's immune system can easily recognize these few antigens and make antibodies to the diseases without getting sick.

- Autism. It has been proven that vaccines do NOT cause autism. The age that children first start showing signs and can be tested for autism is 15-24 months. This is the same age that children receive booster vaccines, so it is understandable that some parents think they are related. I assure you, they are not.

- Long-term protection. Vaccines will protect a person for just as long as if they got the original disease. So a person who had chickenpox as a child is just as protected from getting it again as a person who has received the chickenpox vaccine.

- Mercury. There used to be a preservative called thimerosal in vaccines. That preservative (which contains mercury) has been removed from all vaccines in the US that children receive. The only vaccine that still contains thimerosal is the adult flu vaccine.

- Unnatural exposure. Some people worry that getting exposed to a disease through an injection is not the same as getting it "naturally" by being exposed to a sick person. This is not true; any disease will get into your bloodstream, which is where it is recognized by the body, and once in there the body has no idea how it got in. So getting an injection looks exactly the same to your immune system as getting the disease from a sick person.

If Your Child is Not Completely Vaccinated

Some children are unable to be vaccinated for medical reasons, religious reasons, or personal reasons. When a child has not completed the series of vaccines as laid out by the CDC, it is imperative that the child's parents and doctor keep an eye out for symptoms of certain diseases. Some of the vaccine-preventable diseases mimic common diseases and may accidentally be overlooked, depriving your child of timely, effective treatment.

If your child has not been fully vaccinated, here are some reasons to call a doctor:

- Fever with a rash

- A bulging fontanel (soft spot) in infants or a headache with stiff neck (inability to touch the chin to the chest) in children older than 1 year

- Jaundice (yellow color of the skin and eyes) after age 2 weeks

- Severe watery diarrhea

- Swelling of the parotid glands (near the angle of the jaw) and/or testicle(s)

- Flu-like symptoms (fever, cough, fatigue, sore throat, vomiting/diarrhea, etc.)

Chapter 7

Say Goodbye to Tummy Troubles

It's important to burp your baby often to help reduce spit-ups, gas, and colic.

Why Babies Get Gas

Newborns swallow a lot of air when they eat. If they are not burped in the middle of a feeding, the air builds up into a big bubble in their stomach. When that bubble tries to come out as a burp later, it often brings up a lot of breastmilk or formula with it, causing a large spit-up. Burping your baby during and after a feeding can help to reduce this.

If the burps don't come out, the air may pass into the intestines and cause gas cramps. Have you ever had gassy intestinal cramps? If you have, you know how painful it can be. Babies get symptoms of colic from gas buildup in their intestines.

How to Burp a Baby

First put a burp cloth over your shoulder, just in case any food comes out. Rest your baby against your shoulder. Then cup your hand, like in the picture on the next page, and firmly pat your baby's back. You should pat hard enough that it makes a hollow drum-like sound. It should not make a slapping sound. You can try patting on your own chest for practice, to see how hard to do it. Keep patting your baby's back until you hear a nice, loud burp. Many babies will make other noises like tiny burps or coos that may trick you - wait for that really loud burp before you go back to feeding!

Frequent burping is the #1 way to decrease spit-ups, gas, and colic. Babies with any of these symptoms should burp about 2-3 times per feed.

Bottle-fed babies should be burped after every ounce, and breastfed babies should be burped once every 5 minutes. If you are breastfeeding and your baby is latched tightly and needs to be burped, put a clean finger in the corner of your baby's mouth to break the seal.

How Foods Affect Your Breastfeeding Baby

Some foods in your diet may cause your baby to have gas or colic symptoms. The most common culprits are cruciferous vegetables, beans, garlic, and caffeine. If your baby seems to have intermittent colic, keep a food diary to track what you ate 2-3 meals prior to the symptoms. This can help you to narrow down what foods and beverages in your diet may be affecting your baby.

Food allergies tend to occur in babies who have family members with allergies, asthma, and eczema. The most common food allergies in children are milk, eggs, soy, wheat, fish, shellfish, nuts, and peanuts. The one that is most likely to cause symptoms in breastfeeding babies is milk (which means all dairy products - cheese, yogurt, ice cream, butter, and even milk chocolate).

Food proteins can take days to weeks to clear completely from your system. This means that if you are eliminating a food from your diet, you must avoid it completely for several weeks before it will make a difference. Check with your doctor before eliminating foods from your diet.

How to Treat Colic

Almost all babies get colic; some worse than others. There are tricks at home that you can do to reduce colic, in addition to frequent burping to reduce gas. All babies respond differently, so try each of them to see which helps your baby the most. These colic tricks are:

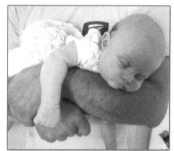

- **Tummy time** - place your baby tummy-down on a blanket for 15-30 minutes twice a day. Always supervise your baby during tummy time. You can also hold your baby in this position (like in the picture) to allow gas to escape. You can see this baby was so happy being held this way that she fell asleep!

- **Bicycle legs** - place your baby face up, then hold your baby's feet and move the legs as if riding a bicycle.

- **Belly massage** - rub your baby's belly slowly in a clockwise direction.

- **Back rubs** - rub in a counterclockwise direction.

Colic usually peaks around 4-6 weeks of age, around the same time as discoordinate stooling. For more information on discoordinate stooling, see the section on constipation in Chapter 4.

Medicines for Colic

Medicines for colic should be used sparingly. They are reserved for when other methods have failed. Check with your doctor before starting any of these medications.

Simethicone (sometimes called baby gas drops) is a medication that can be purchased over-the-counter and may also be prescribed by your doctor. Simethicone is a very safe medication that is not absorbed at all in the intestines. It works by breaking up large gas bubbles into smaller ones that can pass through the intestines more easily, thereby decreasing gas pain. It comes with a little dropper and can be given as needed before meals, up to 12 times per day.

"Gripe water" is a general term for many different preparations that supposedly treat colic. None of the preparations of gripe water are regulated by the FDA, and some contain alcohol or other dangerous ingredients, so please be sure to read the ingredients and/or check with a doctor before giving gripe water to your baby.

Chamomile, licorice, and mint tea are helpful for adults and older children with tummy aches. You can try giving your baby small amounts, for example half an ounce to one ounce, once per day.

Reflux and Spit-Ups

Reflux is when the stomach contents travel up into the esophagus. Spit-ups are when these contents come out of the mouth. Gastro-esophageal reflux disease (GERD) is when the reflux is so bad that it causes your baby to lose weight, choke, or have other problems because of reflux.

All babies have reflux, to some degree, because of an under-developed lower esophageal sphincter (LES). The LES is the muscle between the esophagus and the stomach, which keeps the contents of the stomach in place. This is why you can hang upside-down and not have everything you ate come back out of your mouth. Newborns can't do that. The LES matures around age 6-12 months, so reflux and spit-ups are normal until that age.

A spit-up is not forceful, which differentiates it from vomiting. The contents simply slosh up and out. Vomiting involves the abdominal muscles and a retching movement. Projectile vomiting shoots more than two feet away.

There are two main concerns with reflux and spit-ups:

- Inability to gain weight (or even weight loss)
- Aspiration (choking on the spit-up)

Poor weight gain and weight loss occur when babies spit up too much of each meal. The amount of spit-up always looks like a lot, so I encourage parents to measure 2 tablespoons of water or milk, and dump it on a burp cloth and see how large the spill is. You will be surprised at how far the liquid spreads out. This will give you a good idea of how much spit-up is "normal" - if there is more than 2 tablespoons with each feed, your baby might not be holding down enough to gain weight.

Aspiration (choking) occurs when the spit-up reaches a baby's throat and they breathe it back into their windpipe. It does not happen often, but it is important to know that it is possible. Some babies will aspirate without having any contents come out of their mouth. You may notice your baby gagging, coughing, arching the back, or even turning blue (apnea). If you see any of these signs, you should call your doctor.

How to Avoid Reflux and Spit-Ups

- Don't overfeed your baby. This is by far the most important and most common cause of spit-ups. For babies who are exclusively breastfed, it is nearly impossible to overfeed them, since your milk supply will automatically match your baby's needs. For bottle-fed newborns, they should eat 2-3 ounces of formula every 2-3 hours, for a total of 8-10 feeds (about 24 ounces) in 24 hours.

- Burp your baby well during and after each feed. Your baby should have 2-3 loud burps with each feed.

- Use gravity. You can angle the crib/bassinet by putting a phone book under the legs on one side. This will keep your baby's head higher than the stomach, and gravity will help keep stomach contents down. Do not use a pillow or anything else in the crib to prop your baby up; there is a risk of suffocation. Car seats and infant carriers can be used to keep your baby reclined after a meal, but they are not designed for sleeping.

- Avoid bouncing or swinging your baby for at least 20 minutes after they eat.

- Use anti-reflux formula, or thicken your breast milk. This is an option for babies who spit up so much that they are having trouble gaining or maintaining weight. For bottle-fed babies, there are commercial anti-reflux formulas available. For breastfed babies, there are products that thicken breast milk, such as rice cereal and commercial thickeners. These thicker preparations are a little harder for your baby to suck out of a bottle than regular formula or breast milk, and tend to stay down better. Ask your doctor's advice if you are considering thickening your breast milk or using anti-reflux formula.

Chapter 8

The Shocking Truth About Germs

Babies come into contact with germs (viruses, bacteria, and fungi) every day. This chapter focuses on how to keep your baby healthy.

The Newborn Immune System

White blood cells are responsible for fighting infection. The main white blood cells are called B and T cells. B cells produce antibodies, also called immune globulins, which they use to kill germs. There are five types of immune globulins, called IgG, IgE, IgM, IgA, and IgD. They all have slightly different functions. There are two main types of T cells: those who kill germs directly, and those who call other parts of the immune system to the area of infection.

Newborn babies get most of their immunity from their mother, before they are born. The IgG antibodies are passed through the placenta. Over the first six months of life, the maternal antibodies slowly go away and babies start to make their own antibodies, so by 6-12 months of age their immune system is all their own. This is why the primary series of vaccines is finished by 6 months of age; your baby mounts a good immune response while the immune system is developing. The vaccines given at 2, 4, and 6 months help your baby to be protected against the most common serious childhood diseases by the time the passive maternal immunity has gone away.

When babies are breastfed, some IgA antibodies are passed through the breast milk. These antibodies help to protect your baby against infections as long as your baby is breastfeeding. When you kiss your baby, you pick up the germs on your baby's skin. Your body makes antibodies to the viruses, bacteria, and fungi that you and your baby have been exposed to. Then you pass on any necessary antibodies to your baby when you breastfeed. Isn't that neat?

Preventing Illness in the Home

Your immune system is affected by environmental temperature, so make sure your baby's environment is a comfortable temperature. The thermostat at home should be set to 68-70 degrees. Your baby should be dressed in the type of clothing you would be comfortable in, plus one extra thin layer. For normal room temperature, a thin cotton onesie with an outfit over it is perfect. If your baby is only dressed in one layer, a thin blanket can offer additional warmth without overheating them.

Remember to regularly clean the "germiest" places in your home:

- Keep the kitchen counters wiped down after preparing food.

- Wash the toothbrush holder and pet bowls weekly.

- Wipe down surfaces that your hands touch often (computer mouse/keyboard, phone, tablet, remote control, car keys, etc.) after using them or before giving them to your baby.

- Sponges hold onto germs when they are wet, so allow your kitchen sponge to dry completely between uses. If the sponge never dries, you can microwave it or use antibacterial hand soap once every few days to disinfect it.

- Change water filters per consumer guidelines.

Don't Share Germs with Family

Family members should share all kinds of things, but not germs! The best ways to prevent the spread of germs at home are:

- Wash your hands after sneezing, blowing your nose, coughing, eating, and using the restroom

- Cough or sneeze into your elbow, like in the photo to the right.

- Ask friends and family to wash their hands before holding your baby. (Soap and water is better than hand sanitizer.)

- Ask anyone who appears ill (runny nose, feverish, coughing) not to hold the baby today.

- Make sure that all parents, siblings, grandparents, and other caregivers are up to date on their Tdap and flu vaccines.

- Make sure siblings are up to date on HiB and PCV vaccines; these bacteria can cause pneumonia and meningitis in young babies.

- If anyone in the house is sick with a cold, make sure they use their own hand towel.   Towels are the #1 source of spreading a cold virus within a household - when the sick person dries their hands or face on that towel, someone else who uses the same towel picks up the virus.

- If someone wants to hold your baby after they have been smoking, ask them to change their shirt and wash their hands with soap and water. Make sure the smell of smoke is gone before they hold the baby. If you can smell smoke on them, it means that your baby is breathing in smoke particles, and these can predispose your baby to respiratory illness.

Preventing Illness Outside

When thinking about appropriate clothing for the weather, think of an outfit that you would be comfortable in, then add one more thin layer of clothing or a blanket. If you over-wrap your baby, they will overheat, and if you leave your baby under-dressed, they will get too cold.   You can check by feeling your baby's hands; they should not feel too hot or cold to you, but just right.

Babies should avoid crowds until they receive their first vaccines (around age 2 months), or until they are at least 6 months old if you decide not to vaccinate. Places that are considered "crowded" for babies include grocery stores, movie theaters, department stores, family gatherings, airplanes, and elevators.

Remember that people who come to visit may bring germs into the house, and that siblings can bring infections such as strep throat and the common cold home from school.

Any time someone reaches into the baby carriage, they could be spreading germs. This is especially important to remember during flu season (October-May), when flu and respiratory syncitial virus (RSV) are most prevalent. RSV causes a minor cold in adults and children over 2 years of age, but the younger a child is, the more sick they can become from RSV. Small babies sometimes need to be hospitalized from RSV infections.

Pertussis (whooping cough) is an infection that causes cough and cold symptoms in adults but can cause infants less than 6 months old to stop breathing. Pertussis doesn't have a season, exposure can happen year-round.

The Hygiene Hypothesis

The hygiene hypothesis is this: when a person's immune system doesn't come into contact with enough germs in childhood, it gets "bored" and eventually starts attacking itself, and the person ends up developing allergies or autoimmune diseases. To prevent this, your baby needs to come into contact with a little bit of dirt and germs in order to fight them off and become stronger. But too many germs and your baby can get sick. You need to find the right balance.

DO:

- Use regular soap and water (not antibacterial soap) to clean your hands.

- Keep the house as clean as possible, using baby-safe cleaning products.

- Stay away from anyone who looks very ill, and ask sick family members to wash their hands often and wear a mask around the baby if they are coughing.

- Keep a dog if nobody is allergic. Studies show that babies who grow up with indoor/outdoor dogs get fewer upper respiratory infections, ear infections, and antibiotic treatments than those without dogs.

- Exclusively breastfeed your baby for at least the first 4-6 months, if possible.

DON'T:

- Use hand sanitizer all the time. It doesn't clean your hands or remove dirt, it just kills most of the bacteria and may cause the surviving bacteria to become resistant.

- Boil the pacifier every time it falls on the floor. Seriously you'll go insane. Also, a recent study showed that children whose parents licked off the pacifier before giving it back (as opposed to those who boiled it) had children who got less illnesses and less allergies in childhood.

- Bring your baby into large crowds before 6 months of age. This includes movie theaters, grocery stores, and on airplanes. If you must bring your baby into one of these places, you can put a face mask on your baby to help reduce the chance of getting sick.

- Share hand towels, cups, or utensils with sick family members, or allow sick family members to kiss baby on the face or hands.

Is My Baby Sick?

Infants don't always get the same symptoms as adults when they get sick. Look through Chapter 12 for a list of reasons to call the doctor.

If your baby has a fever (temperature higher than 100.4°F) and is less than 6 months old, you need to take your baby to the nearest Emergency Room. Babies have weak immune systems and have trouble mounting enough of an immune response to get a fever, so if they are able to get a fever, it usually means they are pretty sick.

Other signs of illness in babies are subtle, because they occur in sick babies and sometimes in healthy babies too. Babies with multiple signs are more likely to have an illness than those with only one. Here are some signs that your baby might be sick:

- Cough

- Runny nose, nasal congestion

- Eating less

- Peeing less than usual, or less than 6 times per day

- Vomiting

- Diarrhea

- Fussiness

Chapter 9

The Most Common Rashes and Skin Manifestations

Here are some conditions you can look for.
Some need to be treated, but many are
completely normal!

Jaundice

Newborn jaundice is very common, affecting more than half of newborns. Every baby is born with too many maternal red blood cells. These extra cells get broken down and hemoglobin is released, which is converted into bilirubin, which is what makes a baby's skin turn yellow. Newborn jaundice will occur in the first 2 weeks of life, if it's going to occur at all. On the right, you can see a photo of a newborn with jaundice.

Babies clear bilirubin at different rates, and most bilirubin is cleared in their stool. Over half of all newborns will eat lots and stool plenty and have nothing to worry about. The rest need a little extra help clearing their bilirubin out of their bodies.

The doctor may do a test called a transcutaneous (TC) bilirubin check. The

TC bili is done with a light sensor on your baby's skin, and doesn't hurt at all. It is really just a machine that says how yellow the baby's skin looks to the machine's eye. Of course, skin pigment may interfere with the result of this test. That is why a blood test (serum bilirubin) is used to confirm the TC result, and sometimes is the only test done at all. The serum bilirubin gives the most accurate number of how much bilirubin is in your baby's blood. A level around 10 mg/dl will make a baby's skin appear yellow.

Over the first few days, a baby is supposed to have a little bit of bilirubin in their blood. But if the level gets too high or rises too fast, your doctor may decide to start treatment. A level over 20 is considered dangerous, and can cause brain damage and seizures. In preemies, a level over 16 can be dangerous. But don't worry, treatment is usually started long before the bilirubin level gets that high.

The treatment for newborn jaundice is called phototherapy. Your baby will be placed under blue lights that look a lot like a tanning bed, but they do not emit UV radiation or get hot like tanning beds do. They are simply blue-colored lights, which convert the bilirubin in your baby's skin into a water-soluble form of bilirubin that can be excreted in the urine. Your baby's eyes will be protected from the bright lights with an eye patch.

At home, you can take measures to help prevent jaundice. For the first two weeks of life, when you are about to feed your baby, do this. Remove all of your baby's clothing except for the diaper, and sit (indoors) in a patch of sunlight while you feed your baby. The sunlight will help to break down the bilirubin in your baby's skin. Even if your baby doesn't appear yellow or jaundiced, this will help prevent the development of jaundice in your newborn.

It's important to keep an eye on your newborn for the first 2 weeks to see if the skin or eyes are looking a bit yellow. To check the skin, lightly press on your baby's chest and compare your skin color against your baby's. A normal baby should be paler and pinker than you. If your baby looks yellowish or orange, or has a yellow tint in the whites of the eyes, you should call your doctor.

Diaper Rash

A normal diaper rash, such as the one in the photo below, will respond to over-the-counter diaper creams. But when the diaper rash isn't getting better, or is getting worse with regular diaper cream, your baby may need a medicated cream. Diaper rashes frequently get infected with Candida, a yeast that lives normally on the skin. When there is a break in your baby's skin (during a rash), the Candida can enter and begin to multiply. The dark, moist environment inside a diaper is perfect for the yeast to grow.

A candida diaper rash is a bright red rash around your baby's genitals that has small satellite lesions. The satellite lesions may appear as small red dots, or may coalesce into more complex shapes. This rash tends to be painful, and your baby may cry when you clean the area with washcloths or baby wipes.

Treatment of infected diaper rash includes:

1. Using a medicated cream, ointment, or powder with each diaper change.

2. Continued use of a barrier cream (over-the-counter diaper rash cream).

3. Minimizing the amount of time baby remains in a wet or soiled diaper.

4. Allowing baby to be supervised without a diaper for short periods of time.

Seborrheic Dermatitis (Cradle cap)

This skin condition is most common in the first 6 weeks of life, but can occur up to the first year. It appears on the scalp and eyebrows as greasy, flaky, white to yellow plaques that are stuck to the skin below them. It is more common in children with relatives who have allergies, eczema, and asthma. Treatment is to keep the scalp very moisturized with greasy emollients; you can put olive oil, coconut oil, or petroleum jelly on the scalp before bedtime, then comb baby's hair in the morning. The comb should gently remove some of the greasy patches. With continued application of emollients and gentle combing, baby's skin should return to normal. This process may take several days, even weeks. When the rash is gone, you may need to continue emollients at bedtime to prevent return of the rash. On the right is a photo of a baby with seborrheic dermatitis.

If your baby has seborrheic dermatitis, you should let your doctor know about it. There's no need to make a special appointment, it's just worth mentioning because there may be a risk of infection. Also babies with seborrheic dermatitis are at increased risk of diaper rash.

Eczema

Eczema is very common in babies, especially those with a family member who has asthma, allergies, or eczema. It starts off as a dry patch of skin, typically on areas that rub against the bed or clothing (such as the backs of the arms and the cheeks). But it can occur anywhere on the body. In the photo to the right, you can see a baby with eczema on the forehead and ear.

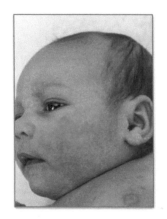

Eczema is itchy, and may cause your baby to scratch or just to be fussy (especially in babies too young to scratch themselves).

The mainstay of treatment for eczema is keeping the skin moisturized. You can bathe your baby once or twice a week with unscented baby soap, and use an unscented greasy emollient (such as petroleum) after the bath.

Continue to apply unscented moisturizing ointment several times a day; I recommend keeping the moisturizer on the changing table and using it each time you change a diaper.

If your baby's eczema is severe and/or does not respond to aggressive moisturizing, you may need a medicated cream, and it may be an indication that your baby has food allergies. Check with your pediatrician if your baby has severe eczema.

Normal Newborn Rash

The baby on the right has a normal newborn rash, or erythema toxicum neonatorum. This rash appears in the first 2-5 days of life, and lasts less than 2 weeks. The rash appears on the face, trunk, and extremities, and is characterized by small bumps surrounded by redness. It looks a bit like small pimples, but is all over the body. It will resolve spontaneously without treatment. There is no need for concern, as it is not harmful and does not bother your baby. Bathing your baby and using baby lotions, oils, and creams may make the rash more apparent but will not make it better or worse.

Pustular Melanosis

This rash starts in the first 1-3 days of life, and only lasts a few days. It looks a lot like the normal newborn rash - small raised bumps surrounded by redness (like pimples) - but when the small bumps pop, clear fluid comes out, and a brown spot that looks like a freckle remains. The brown spots may be present for several weeks or months. This is more common in babies with darker skin.

This rash is not dangerous or uncomfortable, and does not require treatment. Do not scratch or try to burst the bumps yourself, as that can hurt your baby. Don't worry, the bumps and the freckles will go away on their own.

Port Wine Stain

A port wine stain is a flat, dark red spot that is present at birth. Most of these are on the face. They are typically not dangerous, but should be brought to your doctor's attention because they can be associated with other conditions.

Port wine stains don't grow rapidly, they will stay the same size relative to the body as your baby grows. There is no need for treatment, but some families choose to treat the port wine stain with laser surgery for cosmetic reasons.

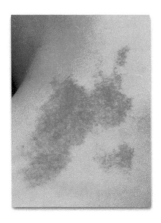

Infantile Hemangioma

A hemangioma is a bright red, lumpy spot composed of many tiny capillaries. It can be present anywhere on the body. Hemangiomas have a tendency to grow quickly before 6 months of age, then slowly shrink up and eventually disappear during elementary school.

Hemangiomas on the face are sometimes treated with medication or laser surgery, especially if they are in a place where they could obstruct breathing or vision (such as the one in the photo to the right).

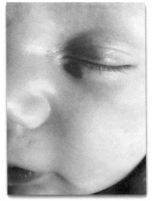

Hemangiomas on the torso can be associated with other, internal hemangiomas. If your baby has a hemangioma on the torso, your doctor will probably want to use an ultrasound machine to check whether there are any on the internal organs.

Salmon Patches

Also called angel kisses on the forehead (as in the picture on the right), or stork bites on the back of the neck, salmon patches are often apparent at birth, and may even appear later.

They can appear anywhere on the body, and babies typically only have one or a few. These flat, irregularly-shaped, salmon-colored spots can vary in size, and are not dangerous. They may appear darker when your baby cries.

Salmon patches on the face tend to fade with age, while those on the back of the neck and other parts of the body do not.

Baby Acne

Babies are exposed to a high dose of maternal hormones in-utero and during breastfeeding, and this can cause some babies to develop acne on their face, chest, and/or back. Baby acne looks like teenage acne and can last anywhere from a few days to several months.

This baby in the photo has acne on the face and chest.

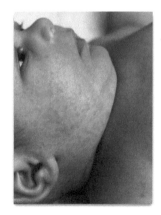

It will resolve on its own without scarring, but if you are concerned, you may ask your doctor about starting treatment. Do not try any adult acne medications, including creams, lotions, face washes, or oral medications, as these can be very harmful to your baby. And do not pick or squeeze the lesions. They will go away on their own.

Milia

Milia are tiny white bumps that appear on a baby's face, and are especially common on the nose and forehead. This baby has milia across the bridge of the nose and cheeks.

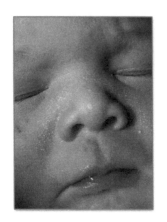

Milia is not dangerous or contagious; it is formed by skin cells that are trapped in small cysts under the skin. There is no treatment necessary; the bumps will resolve on their own in the first few months of life.

Do not pick at the bumps or try to squeeze them out; that can hurt your baby and may cause scarring.

Mongolian Spot

This bluish-gray spot is usually found on the lower back and buttocks, but may also be found on the trunk or extremities. Sometimes several spots are present in the same baby.

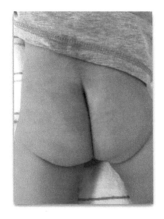

Mongolian spots are more commonly in babies of Asian, African, Hispanic, or Mediterranean descent.

A Mongolian spot looks like a bruise, except that it does not fade into the surrounding skin. It is not dangerous and does not require treatment, but your doctor should be aware if your baby has a Mongolian spot, as these marks can sometimes be confused with bruises of child abuse.

Chapter 10

Circumcision
Pros and Cons

The decision of whether to circumcise your son is a personal one. Here are some pros and cons to help you decide.

Benefits of Circumcision

There is no medical indication for newborn circumcision. The main benefit is a cosmetic outcome. The most common reason parents decide to circumcise their child is because another family member is circumcised, and they want the new baby to look like other family members.

Benefits of circumcision include:

- Cosmetic outcome
- Prevention of phimosis (inability to retract the foreskin), paraphimosis (inability to return retracted foreskin to its original position), and balanoposthitis (inflammation of the foreskin and penis)
- Decreased risk of urinary tract infection
- Decreased risk of sexually transmitted infections
- Decreased risk of penile cancer

Risks of Circumcision

Circumcision is generally very safe, and complications are rare. However, there are some risks associated with circumcision.

Risks include:

- Poor cosmetic outcome (you might not like the way it turns out)

- Bleeding, which can be life-threatening if your baby has hemophilia or another clotting disorder

- Infection at the site of incision

How the Circumcision is Done

There are three main methods used to circumcise newborns. They are named after the clamp used: Mogen, Plastibell, and Gomco. They all start the same way.

Your baby will be placed on his back and his arms and legs will be secured. For anesthesia, the doctor may inject lidocaine at the base of the penis (a dorsal penile block), and/or have your baby consume sugar water (sugar causes a flood of endorphins which act as natural painkillers). Then a blunt probe is placed between the foreskin and the head of the penis (the glans) to separate them. At birth the foreskin is stuck to the glans, so this removes those adhesions.

1. **Mogen clamp** - The foreskin is lifted and the device is placed over the foreskin and pressed closed. It clamps the skin down as it slices through, pressing the blood vessels down to control bleeding. Then the foreskin is pinched open again and the glans appears and it's done. Pros: it's by far the quickest method and least surgical-looking, so it is the one most commonly done in ritual circumcision by mohels. Cons: the device doesn't control the shape of the cut (so it can end up angled or too high or low; the practitioner needs to have practice to make it come out looking nice), risk of bleeding, and there is nothing protecting the glans (so the tip of

the penis itself might actually get cut).

2. **Plastibell** - the foreskin is held up and a slit is made on the top side of the foreskin, so it can be pulled back and the whole glans visualized (to make sure the foreskin is totally separated). Then a plastic ring is placed between the glans and the foreskin, and tied on very tightly with suture. Over the course of several days or a week, the skin between the suture and the ring dies and the plastic device falls off. The hole in the center of the ring allows your baby to pee while it's healing. Pros: the glans is protected, low risk of bleeding, and the device ensures a circular shape to the removed foreskin. Cons: the penis/foreskin typically gets pretty inflamed as it's healing, it can be scary when the device falls off in the diaper, it takes up to a week for the circumcision to be completed.

3. **Gomco** - starts like the plastibell - the foreskin is held up and a slit is made on the top side of the foreskin, so it can be pulled back and the whole glans visualized (to make sure the foreskin is totally separated). Then a metal bell-shaped device is placed between the glans and the foreskin, to protect the glans. The rest of the gomco device is applied onto and around the metal bell - it kind of looks like a stapler or a clamp - and is screwed down tightly to press the blood vessels in the foreskin down to prevent bleeding. The foreskin is removed with a scalpel along the bottom edge of the bell. The device is removed and the circumcision is done. Pros: glans is protected, circumcision is done all at once, device ensures a circular shape to the removed foreskin. Cons: takes about 15-30 minutes, risk of bleeding.

How to Care for the Circumcised Penis

Your doctor should give you instructions for how to take care of your son's penis after circumcision. If your son had a Plastibell circumcision, there is no special care; you simply wait for the plastic ring to fall off, and the healing process is over. This typically happens within a week of the circumcision.

For Mogen or Gomco circumcisions, your son has an open wound that will heal over the course of a few days. While the wound is healing you need to take care that it doesn't stick to the diaper. Have you ever had a scrape stick to the bandaid as it was healing? Ouch. This is the same idea. Each time you finish changing his diaper, put a generous amount of petroleum jelly over the tip of the penis, then place a piece of gauze or a cotton cosmetic pad over the petroleum. Then close the diaper as usual. Your son will be able to pee through the gauze or cosmetic pad without any problems, and the wound will be protected as it heals.

How to Care for the Uncircumcised Penis

The uncircumcised (or intact) penis should be washed gently with soap and water during bath time, and wiped during diaper changes. There is no need to retract the foreskin; only clean what is visible. A way to remember this is "When intact, don't retract. Only clean what can be seen."

Over time, the foreskin will become more retractile and you will eventually be able to see the entire glans. This can take several years, so be patient and don't ever try to forcibly retract the foreskin. As your son grows up, teach him to clean himself during bath time and the risk of urinary tract infections will be minimized.

Chapter 11

Parental Well-Being

Normal Postpartum Mood Swings

Both parents are prone to mood swings after the birth of the baby. One main reason for this is lack of sleep. For at least the first 2 weeks, your baby will wake up every few hours and cry and need to eat and be changed. This interrupted sleep pattern can wear on both parents and cause irritability and short fuses. See chapter 5 for more information on getting more sleep.

Another reason for mood swings is low blood sugar. It's common for new parents to forget to eat, since their new baby is so engrossing. It can help to keep healthy snacks around the house, near places you sit often. This way you can eat something quick when you start to feel out of sorts.

Remember, having a new baby is a difficult adjustment for both parents. Hang in there; the hard times will pass.

Baby Blues

It is common to feel sad or moody after giving birth, due to the massive hormonal shifts that take place. Up to 80% of new moms will experience baby blues. Symptoms of baby blues include crying for no reason, feeling overwhelmed, impatience, irritability, anxiety, fatigue, insomnia, sadness, poor concentration, and mood changes. The symptoms usually come and go, lasting for minutes to hours each day, and disappear by the time your baby is 2 weeks old. A mom with baby blues is able to function normally and take care of herself and her baby.

Postpartum Depression

About 20% of new moms will experience postpartum depression. Symptoms include feelings of inadequacy, guilt, anxiety, despondency, tearfulness, and feeling detached from your baby.

Postpartum depression can occur up until your baby is a year old, and the symptoms can creep up so slowly that you might not notice them.

The Edinburgh postnatal depression scale is a tool used to screen for postpartum depression. It has ten questions asking how you have been feeling over the past week. If you aren't sure whether you are experiencing baby blues or postpartum depression, you can take the quiz at the end of this chapter. Note: Users may reproduce this scale without further permission providing they respect the copyright (which remains with the British Journal of Psychiatry), quote the names of the authors and include the title and the source of the paper in all reproduced copies. I have referenced the source on page 103 in the "References" section.

If you ever have thoughts of harming yourself or your baby, talk to your doctor or therapist about it. They will NOT try to take your baby away or report you to authorities. They will help you.

What You Can Do

You can do the following to help minimize your risk of postpartum mood disorders.

- Talk with someone about how you are feeling. A therapist or a good friend can help a lot.

- Eat a healthy diet. Make sure you are remembering to eat, as low blood sugar can really affect your mood.

- Take a hot shower while someone else holds the baby.

- Go outside for at least 20 minutes every day.

- Ask for help with meals, housework, and baby care. Accept help from friends who offer.

- Be kind to yourself. Becoming a parent is one of the most difficult things in the world. If you're reading this book I know you care about your baby and that tells me you're already doing a great job!

- Remember that everything is a phase and will pass. Each phase has its own difficulties and its own joys. Try to focus on the positive!

The Edinburgh Postnatal Depression Scale

This scale is used by many doctors to screen for postpartum depression. Select the answer that best suits the way you have been feeling for the past week, and add up the total points at the end.

A score of 1-8 points is likely to be normal baby blues and postpartum mood swings. A score of 9-10 is means you should repeat the test in a week, but call your doctor if you start feeling worse. A score of 11 or more means you should call your doctor, because you are probably suffering from postpartum depression. Also, if you score anything other than 0 on question 10, you should call your doctor right away.

Here are the questions:

1. I have been able to laugh and see the funny side of things
   - ☐ (0) As much as I always could
   - ☐ (1) Not quite so much now
   - ☐ (2) Definitely not so much now
   - ☐ (3) Not at all

2. I have looked forward with enjoyment to things
   - ☐ (0) As much as I ever did
   - ☐ (1) Rather less than I used to
   - ☐ (2) Definitely less than I used to
   - ☐ (3) Hardly at all

3. I have blamed myself unnecessarily when things went wrong
   - ☐ (0) No, never
   - ☐ (1) Not very often
   - ☐ (2) Yes, some of the time
   - ☐ (3) Yes, most of the time

4. I have been anxious or worried for no good reason
   - ☐ (0) No, not at all
   - ☐ (1) Hardly ever
   - ☐ (2) Yes, sometimes
   - ☐ (3) Yes, often

5. I have felt scared or panicky for no good reason
   - ☐ (0) No, not at all
   - ☐ (1) No, not much
   - ☐ (2) Yes, sometimes
   - ☐ (3) Yes, quite a lot

6. Things have been getting to me
   - ☐ (0) No, I have been coping as well as ever
   - ☐ (1) No, most of the time I have coped quite well
   - ☐ (2) Yes, sometimes I haven't been coping as well as usual
   - ☐ (3) Yes, most of the time I haven't been able to cope at all

7. I have been so unhappy that I have had difficulty sleeping
   - ☐ (0) No, not at all
   - ☐ (1) No, not very often
   - ☐ (2) Yes, sometimes
   - ☐ (3) Yes, most of the time

8. I have felt sad or miserable
   - ☐ (0) No, not at all
   - ☐ (1) Not very often
   - ☐ (2) Yes, quite often
   - ☐ (3) Yes, most of the time

9. I have been so unhappy that I've been crying
   - ☐ (0) No, never
   - ☐ (1) Only occasionally
   - ☐ (2) Yes, quite often
   - ☐ (3) Yes, most of the time

10. The thought of harming myself has occurred to me*
    - ☐ (0) Never
    - ☐ (1) Hardly ever
    - ☐ (2) Sometimes
    - ☐ (3) Yes, quite often
      *Remember - anything other than 0 on this question means you need to call your doctor!

Chapter 12

Reasons to Call

Your Doctor NOW

*All of these conditions are rare, but they
are reasons to seek immediate medical
attention for your baby.*

Most of these conditions have already been mentioned in the
book. I put them together into one chapter for easier reference.

Abnormal Temperature

You should have a rectal thermometer at home. Go buy one if
you don't have one yet. The rectal temperature is the most
accurate in babies, since their skin doesn't hold heat very well. If
your baby is acting strange, or feels especially warm or cool to
the touch, you can check a rectal temperature.

A rectal temperature higher than 100.4 degrees Fahrenheit (38
degrees Celsius) is considered a fever. A rectal temperature less
than 96 degrees Fahrenheit (35.5 degrees Celsius) is considered
to be hypothermia.

Babies who are less than 6 months old have immature immune systems, and an abnormal temperature (either high or low) can be a sign that they have an infection. If your baby has an abnormal temperature measured with a thermometer, you ned to call a doctor.

Apnea/Cyanosis

If your baby appears to stop breathing for several seconds (apnea), or starts turning blue (cyanosis), it's time to call a doctor. Cyanosis is most apparent on and around the lips, fingertips, and toes.

Aspiration/Choking

Signs of aspiration/choking include gagging, coughing, arching the back, vomiting, and turning blue. Call your doctor if your baby is experiencing these symptoms.

Blood in the Diaper

If you see blood in your baby's diaper, and you think it is coming from the urine or stool (and not from pseudomenses), call the doctor. There is more information about pseudomenses in Chapter 4.

Bulging Fontanel

If the anterior fontanel (soft spot) seems to be higher than the rest of the skull, this is a sign that the pressure around your baby's brain is too high. The fontanel will often raise during crying, straining to poo, and other normal maneuvers. That is nothing to worry about. But when the fontanel is bulging when your baby is calm, you need to see a doctor.

Diarrhea/Vomiting

Babies can get dehydrated very quickly from diarrhea and/or vomiting. See Chapters 4 and 7 for definitions of true diarrhea and vomiting.

Head injury

Any time your baby falls off a surface (couch, changing table, bed, etc.) you need to call a doctor to make sure your baby did not sustain a concussion.

Signs of concussion include:

• Losing consciousness / fainting

• Vomiting

• Change in personality - persistent crying, acting strange, trouble sleeping/eating, etc.

• Pupils unequal size

• Seizure

• Weakness of the entire body or parts of the body

Jaundice

If your baby's skin and eyes appear yellow, you should call a doctor. Most babies will have jaundice at some point, and your doctor can do a test to determine the level of bilirubin in the blood to see whether the jaundice needs treatment or not. If the level of bilirubin is too high and is not treated, it can cause brain damage.

Seizure

Infantile seizures may be the whole body (generalized shaking and tremors), or may only involve part of the body. Some signs of seizures are:

- The whole body makes repetitive jerking movements

- One or two extremities make repetitive jerking movements

- Sucking when there is nothing in the mouth

- Fast blinking

If you think your baby might be having a seizure, remove anything that might be in baby's mouth, make sure your baby is not left unattended on a surface, and call an ambulance.

Umbilical Cord Infection

If the skin around the umbilical cord is red, swollen, warm to touch, and tender, these are signs of infection.

Umbilical Granuloma

When the umbilical cord falls off, it's normal to have a little bit of bleeding and what looks like yellowish goo. After the cord has fallen off, clean the area gently with a wet washcloth or a cotton ball with rubbing alcohol. The bleeding should stop immediately, and much of the yellow goo will come off. If the umbilicus is still bleeding, or there is too much yellowness, there may be an umbilical granuloma in there. This can be treated easily at the doctor's office with a chemical called silver nitrate. The chemical cauterizes the granuloma, and the process is completely painless for your baby.

Afterword

The Adventure Begins!

After reading this book, you should have all of the basic information needed to care for your new baby.

If you have a medical question, please ask a medical professional, rather than looking on the internet for answers. The type of medical information that is found online tends to highlight the most extreme, severe, and unlikely cases, and does not help the majority of families. Online pictures of rashes and other manifestations of disease are often worst-case scenarios.

As a new parent, you're going to get all kinds of advice on how to raise your baby, whether you ask for it or not. You will get advice from your relatives, your partner's relatives, friends, doctors, nurses, teachers, and even strangers you come across. But no matter what anyone says, it is up to YOU to raise your baby how you see fit. It may be difficult, but sometimes the best answer to disagreeable advice is simply to nod your head and say, "OK," and then continue to raise your child how you want.

My final piece of advice is this: enjoy every moment with your baby. They grow up fast.

Common Questions

You may have wondered this yourself

Q: How can I tell if my baby is cold? Isn't is safer to just add extra layers or a blanket?

A: You can check by feeling your baby's hands, feet, and nose. Infants have a hard time thermoregulating (maintaining a normal body temperature), and they can overheat if they are wrapped in a heavy blanket. Your baby needs about one more thin layer of clothing than an adult to be a comfortable temperature (a onesie under a regular outfit is plenty).

Q: Can I wait to vaccinate my child? Isn't that a lot of shots for their tiny immune system?

A: Vaccines are proven to be safe and effective, and prevent dangerous diseases. The point of vaccinating your baby is to prevent the diseases that are most likely to present harm. Vaccines are spread out to protect children at the ages they need them most. There has been extensive research by the CDC (Center for Disease Control) to make sure that vaccines given to babies will cause them to have antibodies long enough to fight off the diseases they come into contact with. Even if a mother has had a vaccine-preventable disease, she cannot pass enough antibodies for that disease through breast milk, and the baby should be vaccinated.

Q: *When can I give honey to my baby?*
    A: Honey is not safe for children until they are 1 year old. Honey sometimes contains spores of Clostridium botulinum, the bacteria that causes botulism (a deadly disease). After one year of age, a baby can produce enough stomach acid to kill off the spore. For children aged 1 year and older, honey can be used as a safe and effective cough suppressant.

Q: *What medicines can I give to my baby for pain and fever?*
    A: Acetaminophen (Tylenol) is safe in infants of all ages. Ibuprofen (Aleve, Motrin) is approved for babies who are 6 months and older. Aspirin is NOT safe for children, it is only safe in adults 19 years and older. In children with viral illness, aspirin can cause Reye syndrome, which causes liver and brain damage (and can be deadly).

Q: *Can I use a cold bath to bring down a fever?*
    A: No. A cold bath will make your child feel worse, shiver more, and can worsen the fever. A fever happens because the body's thermostat is set too high. Fever medicines (acetaminophen or ibuprofen) reset the body's thermostat to normal. Lukewarm baths or cool compresses (a damp washcloth on the forehead or belly) can be used in conjunction with fever medicines; they cool the body from the outside as the medicine lets it return to normal from the inside. If you only use external cooling methods without resetting the thermostat, the body keeps trying to have a fever. It's like if your house were too hot and you opened the doors but left the thermostat set to high - the heater keeps running trying to keep the house hot. You need to turn off the heater and then open the doors to cool the house.

Q: *Why do we vaccinate for chicken pox? Nobody ever died of chicken pox right?*
    A: School-age children who get chicken pox usually only get a mild illness, but babies who get chicken pox can die from it. If a pregnant woman gets chicken pox during the pregnancy, it can cause her baby to have birth defects,

and she might even have a miscarriage.
Chicken pox is contagious 2 days before the rash, and until all the lesions have crusted over, usually 5-7 days after the rash begins.

Q: Why can't I let my baby sleep face down or sideways?
A: Both face-down and side-sleeping positions are shown to increase the risk of SIDS (sudden infant death syndrome / crib death). It is safest to place your baby face up to sleep, on a flat surface (in a crib or bassinet). Once your baby is old enough to roll over, you can allow your baby to sleep in other positions during the night, but you should still put your baby face up to sleep at the beginning of the night.

Q: How long do I need to swaddle my baby?
A: Swaddling is for comfort, so if your baby keeps busting out of a swaddle, it is time to stop. If your baby loves being swaddled, you can wait until your baby is old enough to roll over.

Q: What do I need to worry about in terms of choking hazards?
A: Peanuts, popcorn, hot dogs, and grapes are the most common foods that are choking hazards in children under age 3. One way to avoid choking is to make sure your baby sits at a table while eating - it is not safe to eat while playing, laughing, walking, or running. Small objects (less than the diameter of a quarter in any direction) can also present a choking hazard - if you have an older child at home, keep these toys in a place where your new baby won't be able to reach them.

Q: Is my baby going to get addicted to the pacifier?
A: Young babies will not get addicted to using a pacifier. You can stop offering a pacifier at 9-12 months of age with minimal conflict. If you wait longer than that, your child can become dependent on the pacifier, and it will be more difficult to break the habit. One way to wean children off a pacifier is to cut the tip off, then every few days cut a little more off, until they lose interest. Just go slowly so

they don't start substituting a thumb instead.

Q: Will playing Mozart make my baby smarter?
    A: This has not been proven to be true.

Q: Will the iron in my baby's formula cause constipation?
    A: No, there is not enough iron in formula to cause
    constipation.

Q: Can I add rice cereal at bedtime to help my baby sleep
   through the night?
    A: No, adding rice cereal to the bottle can be dangerous
    and should only be done under your doctor's guidance.
    Newborns need to eat every 2-4 hours, so regardless of
    what you feed them, they should not sleep through the
    night. If your baby sleeps for 4 straight hours, you need to
    wake your baby up to eat.

Q: Does my baby need to avoid milk while ill with diarrhea?
    A: No, keep feeding your baby breast milk or formula even
    if your baby has diarrhea. A child with diarrhea does not
    need any dietary restrictions.

Q: Should I check my baby's temperature in the armpit? That's
how they did it in the hospital.
    A: After the initial newborn period (the first few days), the
    axillary temperature is very inaccurate. It reflects skin
    temperature, and not the core temperature. An infant's
    temperature should be checked rectally for the most
    accurate result. Temporal artery thermometers are a new,
    accurate way to check temperature, when used properly.
    Ear thermometers are not accurate in newborns because
    their ear canals are too small. Oral thermometers cannot
    be used until your child is able to sit still with the
    thermometer under the tongue, which is usually around
    age 5 years. It can be dangerous to try to take an oral
    temperature in a baby.

Appendix B

Baby Lists

What baby items do you really need?
Check out these lists for guidance!

Items to buy Before Baby is Born

Items for mom:

- ☐ Heavy-flow pads or Depends for the bleeding after delivery
- ☐ Comfortable pajamas - button up top if breastfeeding
- ☐ Nursing bras
- ☐ Nursing shirts / tank tops
- ☐ Gel breast pads for comfort
- ☐ Protective nipple covers
- ☐ Nipple cream (and disposable breast pads to protect clothes)
- ☐ A breast pump
- ☐ Hands-free pumping bra

Clothing for Baby:

- ☐ Newborn and 0-3 month size onesies
- ☐ Hats
- ☐ Scratch mittens

☐ Socks

For the changing table:

☐ Diapers

☐ Diaper cream

☐ Diaper cream spatula (optional)

☐ Diaper pail

☐ Changing pad

☐ Wipes

☐ Wipe warmer (optional)

Baby furniture:

☐ A crib, bassinet, and/or co-sleeper

☐ Sheets for the crib, bassinet, and/or co-sleeper

☐ Nursing pillow

☐ Baby seat that allows baby to lie down

☐ Baby swing that allows baby to lie down

☐ Rocking chair or glider

General baby items:

☐ Car seat

☐ Stroller

☐ Thermometer - temporal artery or rectal thermometer

☐ Burp cloths

☐ Nasal bulb suction

☐ Pacifiers

☐ Medicines: acetaminophen, simethicone gas drops, infant tri-vitamins (Vitamin A, C, D), antifungal cream for infected diaper rash, saline nose drops

Items to buy After Baby is Born

Apps and electronics:

☐ An app to track baby's eating, peeing, and pooping

☐ A white noise machine or white noise app

☐ Baby monitor with video

☐ Formula maker

☐ Bottle warmer

☐ Bottle sterilizer

Baby clothing:

☐ Kimono shirts

☐ Long-sleeve, long-leg onesies with zippers

☐ Leg warmers

☐ Sleep sacks

Items for mom:

☐ Breast pads to catch extra milk

☐ Breast milk freezer storage bags

Baby furniture:

☐ Playpen

☐ Baby seat that allows baby to sit upright

☐ A swing where baby can sit upright

General baby items:

☐ Baby bottles

☐ Preemie flow nipples

☐ Baby carrier

☐ Muslin baby blankets

Packing the Diaper Bag

These items are handy to keep in the diaper bag!

- ☐ Diapers
- ☐ Diaper rash cream
- ☐ Wipes
- ☐ Baby clothes (2 outfits + socks)
- ☐ Baby toy(s)
- ☐ Bandaids
- ☐ Burp cloths / washcloths / cloth diapers
- ☐ Changing pad
- ☐ Hand sanitizer
- ☐ Money
- ☐ Muslin blanket
- ☐ Pacifier(s)
- ☐ Pen(s)
- ☐ Shirt for mom (in case of spit ups)
- ☐ Snacks for mom (and baby when old enough)
- ☐ Sunscreen
- ☐ Water bottles
- ☐ Plastic bags for diapers, wet clothes, trash

Newborn Activity Chart

First 2 Weeks

Mark one of the boxes each time your baby eats, pees, and poops. This will help you and your pediatrician know whether your baby is eating enough.

Day	Feeding	Pee	Poop
1	1 2 3 4	1 2 3 4	1 2 3 4
2	1 2 3 4	1 2 3 4	1 2 3 4
3	1 2 3 4 5 6	1 2 3 4 5 6	1 2 3 4 5 6
4	1 2 3 4 5 6 7 8	1 2 3 4 5 6 7 8	1 2 3 4 5 6 7 8
5	1 2 3 4 5 6 7 8 9 0 1 2	1 2 3 4 5 6 7 8 9 0 1 2	1 2 3 4 5 6 7 8 9 0 1 2

6	1 2 3 4 / 5 6 7 8 / 9 0 1 2	1 2 3 4 / 5 6 7 8 / 9 0 1 2	1 2 3 4 / 5 6 7 8 / 9 0 1 2
7	1 2 3 4 / 5 6 7 8 / 9 0 1 2	1 2 3 4 / 5 6 7 8 / 9 0 1 2	1 2 3 4 / 5 6 7 8 / 9 0 1 2
8	1 2 3 4 / 5 6 7 8 / 9 0 1 2	1 2 3 4 / 5 6 7 8 / 9 0 1 2	1 2 3 4 / 5 6 7 8 / 9 0 1 2
9	1 2 3 4 / 5 6 7 8 / 9 0 1 2	1 2 3 4 / 5 6 7 8 / 9 0 1 2	1 2 3 4 / 5 6 7 8 / 9 0 1 2
10	1 2 3 4 / 5 6 7 8 / 9 0 1 2	1 2 3 4 / 5 6 7 8 / 9 0 1 2	1 2 3 4 / 5 6 7 8 / 9 0 1 2
11	1 2 3 4 / 5 6 7 8 / 9 0 1 2	1 2 3 4 / 5 6 7 8 / 9 0 1 2	1 2 3 4 / 5 6 7 8 / 9 0 1 2
12	1 2 3 4 / 5 6 7 8 / 9 0 1 2	1 2 3 4 / 5 6 7 8 / 9 0 1 2	1 2 3 4 / 5 6 7 8 / 9 0 1 2
13	1 2 3 4 / 5 6 7 8 / 9 0 1 2	1 2 3 4 / 5 6 7 8 / 9 0 1 2	1 2 3 4 / 5 6 7 8 / 9 0 1 2
14	1 2 3 4 / 5 6 7 8 / 9 0 1 2	1 2 3 4 / 5 6 7 8 / 9 0 1 2	1 2 3 4 / 5 6 7 8 / 9 0 1 2

Further Reading

*For more information, the author
recommends the following books*

Pregnancy

- *The Girlfriends' Guide to Pregnancy* by Vicki Iovine. This book is lighthearted and fun, and gives great advice based on the experiences of the author and her friends.

- *Great Expectations* by Sandy Jones and Marcie Jones Brennan. This book is far more supportive and less scary than What to Expect, which is truly awful in my opinion.

Babyhood

- *The Baby Book* by Dr. Sears. This book is very long and comprehensive. If you have a question about something your baby is doing, it will probably be in this book. *The Breastfeeding Book* is another good one by Dr. Sears.

- *The No Cry Sleep Solution* by Elizabeth Pantley. This book has many different ideas for helping your child sleep through the night. There is also information about normal sleep architecture, sleep hygiene, co-sleeping safely, and how new parents can combat insomnia.

- The Holistic Pediatrician by Kathi Kemper. This book gives a well-rounded approach to the most common pediatric illnesses, including how to prevent and treat them with western and holistic methods.

Parenting

- *Raising an Emotionally Intelligent Child* by John Gottman. This book provides an entire framework for relating to and interacting with a child throughout the years that respects and honors the child's feelings while helping to develop a strong sense of self, courage, and independence.

- *Parenting from the Inside Out* by Daniel Seigel and Mary Hartzell. This book shows us how our own life experiences affect our parenting, and then how we can consciously address that.

Discipline

- *Parenting With Love and Logic* by Foster Cline and Jim Fay. The Love and Logic method involves giving children more choices and a sense of control in a safe and loving way, to avoid the power struggles that come along with parenting. It's even better to take a Love and Logic class if you can - the class offers examples, handouts, support from other parents, and hilarious video clips.

- *How to Talk So Kids Will Listen and Listen So Kids Will Talk* by Adele Faber and Elaine Mazlish. This book has lots of examples and handy cartoon summaries, so that if one parent reads the book, they can show the other parent the cartoon and both parents will be on the same page.

- *The Discipline Book* by Dr. Sears. This book has lots of creative ideas that help teach rather than punish.

Difficult children

- Raising Your Spirited Child. This book helps parents to better understand how their child operates, and offers many suggestions for how to work with that.

- The Connected Child. This book is meant for adoptive families, but is also helpful for special needs families and blended families.

Siblings

- *Siblings without Rivalry* by Adele Faber and Elaine Mazlish. This book helps you prevent sibling rivalry before it even begins.

References

Following is a list of some of the books and articles whose information was taken into consideration during the writing of The Baby Manual.

- American Academy of Pediatrics. "Policy Statement: Breastfeeding and the Use of Human Milk." *Pediatrics* 2012: e827-41. Web.

- American Academy of Pediatrics. "Management of Hyperbilirubinemia in the Newborn Infant 35 or More Weeks of Gestation." *Pediatrics* 2004: 297-316.

- Bechtel, Kristin. "Pediatric Chickenpox" *Medscape*. Sep 2011. Web.

- Bergroth, E, et al. "Respiratory Tract Illnesses During the First Year of Life: Effect of Dog and Cat Contacts."(2012) *Pediatrics* 2011. Print.

- Borowitz, Stephen. "Constipation." *eMedicine Specialties > Pediatrics > Gastroenterology*. February 2010. Web.

- Boschert, Sherry. "Infant Invasive Pneumococcus." *ACEP news*. Aug 8, 2012. Web.

- Brazelton, T. Berry. *Touchpoints, the Essential Reference.* Reading: Addison Wesley, 1996. Print.

- Carmody, Kristin. "Management of acute Presentation of Mumps." *Medscape*. Sep 2012. Web.

- Colen, Cynthia G., and David M. Ramey. "Is breast truly best? Estimating the effects of breastfeeding on long-term child health and wellbeing in the United States using sibling comparisons." Social Science & Medicine 109 (2014): 55-65. Web.

- Cox, J.L., Holden, J.M. and Sagovsky, R. "Detection of Postnatal Depression: Development of the 10-item Edinburgh Postnatal Depression Scale." British Journal of Psychiatry 150, (1987): 782-786.

- Custer, Jason and Racel Rau. *The Harriet Lane Handbook, 18th ed.* Mosby Elsevier, 2009. Print.

- Danielsson, Bernt, and Carl Philip Hwang. "Treatment of infantile colic with surface active substance (simethicone)." Acta Paediatrica 74.3 (1985): 446-50. Web.

- Devarajan, Vidya. "Hemophilus Influenzae Infections." *Medscape.* Jan 10, 2012. Web.

- Duygu, Arikan, et al. "Effectiveness of massage, sucrose solution, herbal tea or hydrolysed formula in the treatment of infantile colic." Journal of clinical nursing 17.13 (2008): 1754-61. Web.

- Ezike, Elias. "Pediatric Rubella" *Medscape.* Oct 2011. Web.

- Farber, Elaine. *Baby Lists - What to Do and What to Get to Prepare for Baby.* Avon: Adams Media, 2007. Print.

- Fastle, Rebecca, and Joan Bothner. "Lumbar Puncture: Indications, Contraindications, Technique, and Complications in Children." *Up To Date*, May 2010. Web.

- Ferry, George. "Definition, clinical manifestations, and evaluation of functional fecal incontinence in infants and children." *UpToDate.* June 2007. Web.

- Ferry, George. "Patient Information: Constipation in infants and children." *UpToDate.* August 2010. Web.

- Ferry, George. "Treatment of chronic functional constipation and fecal incontinence in infants and children." *UpToDate.* August 2010. Web.

- Garrison, Michelle M., and Dimitri A. Christakis. "A systematic review of treatments for infant colic." Pediatrics 106.Supplement 1 (2000): 184-90. Web.

- Guinto-Ocampo, Hazel."Pertussis." *Medscape.* Aug 16, 2012. Web.

- Hay, William W et al. *Current Diagnosis and Treatment Pediatrics, 19th ed.* Lange McGraw Hill, 2009. Print.

- Hiscock, Harriet, and Melissa Wake. "Randomised controlled trial of behavioural infant sleep intervention to improve infant sleep and maternal mood." Bmj 324.7345 (2002): 1062. Web.

- Iovine, Vicki. *The Girlfriend's Guide to Surviving the First Year of Motherhood.* New York: The Berkley Publishing Group, 1997. Print.

- Javid, Mahmud. "Meningococcemia" *Medscape.* Aug 2012. Web.

- Karp, Harvey. *The Happiest Baby on the Block.* New York: Bantam Dell, 2003. Print.

- Kemper, Kathi. *The Holistic Pediatrician.* New York: Quill, 2002. Print.

- Kwan, M. L., et al. "Breastfeeding, PAM50 Tumor Subtype, and Breast Cancer Prognosis and Survival." *Journal of the National Cancer Institute* 2015: 107 (7): djv0872015-03-31. Web.

- Loening-Baucke, Vera. "Prevalence, symptoms and outcome of constipation in infants and toddlers." The Journal of pediatrics 146.3 (2005): 359-363. Web.

- Lucassen, P. L. B. J., et al. "Effectiveness of treatments for infantile colic: systematic review." Bmj 316.7144 (1998): 1563-8. Web.

- Lunn, Andrew, and Thomas A. Forbes. "Haematuria and proteinuria in childhood." Paediatrics and child health 22.8 (2012): 315-321. Web.

- Maguire, Jonathan et al. "Should a Head-Injured Child Receive a Head CT Scan? A Systematic Review of Clinical Prediction Rules." *Pediatrics* July 2009: Volume 124, Number 1. Web.

- Metcalf, Thomas J., et al. "Simethicone in the treatment of infant colic: a randomized, placebo-controlled, multicenter trial." Pediatrics 94.1 (1994): 29-34. Web.

- Murphy, Elizabeth. "'Breast is best': Infant feeding decisions and maternal deviance." Sociology of Health & Illness 21.2 (1999): 187-208. Web.

- Offit, Paul A. "Vaccine ingredients - Aluminum." *Children's Hospital of Philadelphia*. 2016. Web.

- Osmond, Martin et al. "CATCH: A Clinical Decision Rule for the Use of Computed Tomography in Children with Minor Head Injury." *Canadian Medical Association Journal* March 2010: *Volume 182, Number 4. Web.*

- Parmelee, Arthur H., Waldemar H. Wenner, and Helen R. Schulz. "Infant sleep patterns: from birth to 16 weeks of age." *The Journal of Pediatrics* 65.4 (1964): 576-582. Web.

- Piedra, Pedro and Ann Stark. "Bronchiolitis in infants and children: Treatment; outcome; and prevention." *UpToDate.* September 2010. Web.

- Rajashekhar MM, Groshkova T, Mayet S. Illicit drug use in pregnancy: effects and management. *Expert Review of Obstetrics and Gynecology* 2011: 6(2):179–92. Web.

- Roberts, Ostapchuk, and O'Brien. "Infantile Colic." *American Family Physician*. 15 Aug 2004: 735-40. Web.

- Seavey, Nina. "A Paralyzing Fear: The triumph over Polio in America." Web.

- Shah, Divya K. "Is Breast Always Best?: A Personal Reflection on the Challenges of Breastfeeding." Obstetrics & Gynecology 121.4 (2013): 869-871. Web.

- Skadberg, Britt T., Inge Morild, and Trond Markestad. "Abandoning prone sleeping: Effect on the risk of sudden infant death syndrome." The Journal of pediatrics 132.2 (1998): 340-3. Web.

- Spock, Benjamin and Steven Parker. *Dr. Spock's Baby and Child Care*. New York: First Pocket Books, 1998. Print.

- Tahtinen, Paula et al. "A Placebo-Controlled Trial of Antimicrobial Treatment for Acute Otitis Media." *New England Journal of Medicine* 2011: 116-26. Print.

- Unknown Author. "Baby Poop: A Visual Guide." *Baby Center website*. Aug 2015. Web.

- Unknown Author. "Baby Sleep Basics: Birth to Three Months." *Baby Center website*. April 2015. Web.

- Unknown Author. "Help Your Baby Sleep Through the Night." *Web MD*. April 2015. Web.

- Unknown Author. "Immunization Schedules." *CDC website*. Oct 2015. Web.

- Unknown Author. "Measles." *CDC website*. Oct 2012. Web.

- Unknown Author. "Poliomyelitis." *Pubmed Health online encyclopedia*. Aug 2011. Web.

- Unknown Author. "Rotavirus" *CDC website*. Oct 28, 2010. Web.

- Unknown Author. "Tetanus." *PubMed Health online encyclopedia.* Nov 22, 2011. Web.

- Unknown Author. "Visual Guide to Children's Rashes and Skin Conditions." *Baby Center website.* Oct 2015. Web.

- Unknown Author. "What Baby Pee can Tell You." *Love Your Baby website.* Oct 2015. Web.

- Unknown Author. "When to do a Lumbar Puncture in a Neonate." *Archives of Disease in Childhood*, 1989, vol 64, pp 313-316. Web.

- Van der Wal, M. F., et al. "Mothers' reports of infant crying and soothing in a multicultural population." Archives of disease in childhood 79.4 (1998): 312-317.

- Vernacchio, Louis, et al. "Diarrhea in American infants and young children in the community setting: incidence, clinical presentation and microbiology." The Pediatric infectious disease journal 25.1 (2006): 2-7. Web.

- Wiswell, Thomas, Stephen Baumgart, Catherine Gannon, and Alan Spitzer. "No Lumbar Puncture in the Evaluation for Early Neonatal Sepsis: Will Meningitis Be Missed?" *Pediatrics*, June 1985, Vol 95, No 8. Web.

- Zeretzke, Karen. "Massage for Colic." New Beginnings 15.1 (1998): 13. Web.

- All images in this book are used with written permission of the parents.

Index

A

Acne, newborn, 63
Allergies, 6, 18, 22, 25-26, 33, 46, 54, 59-61
Angel kisses
    see salmon patch
Anti-reflux formula, 22, 49
Anxiety, 14, 69-70
Apnea, 12, 49, 74
Aspirin, 82

B

Baby blues, 69-70
Baby food, 16, 24-27, 31, 33, 83
Baby items, 2, 87-90
Baby registry
    see baby items
Bassinet, 37, 49, 83, 88
Bathing, 9, 10, 12-13, 60-61, 68, 82
Bed, 8, 36-38, 76
    see also bassinet, crib
Bedtime, 35-39, 84
Belly button, 10-11
Bilirubin, 57-58, 75
Birth preparation , 1-5
    signs of labor, 1-2
    what doctors are doing, 4-5
Birth mark, 62-64
    hemangioma, 62
    mongolian spot, 64
    port wine stain, 62
    salmon patch, 63

Blankets , 2, 8, 11, 37, 52-53, 81, 89-90
Bleeding
    belly button, 11, 76
    from circumcision, 66-68
    in diaper, 9, 30-33, 74
    umbilical cord, 11, 76
Blood in diaper, 9, 30-33, 74
Bottle feeding, 15-17, 21-24, 38, 49, 84
    types of formula, 21-22
    how to prepare formula, 23
    how long formula lasts, 23
    overeating, 24
Bottles, 19-24, 38, 89
Botulism, 82
Bowel movements
    see stool
Breast pump, 2, 19-21, 87
    how to choose, 20
    get most pumping, 20-21
Breastfeeding, 15-21
    pros and cons, 16-19
    how long milk lasts, 19-20
    nipple confusion, 27
Breathing patterns, 12, 74
Burping, 24, 45-46, 49
    GER and, 48-49
    how to, 45-46

C

Calcium, 16, 21-22
Calming baby, 12
Car seat, 2, 6, 49, 88

Temperature
  see fever
Tummy time, 47

U

Umbilical cord, 10, 12, 76
Umbilical granuloma, 11, 76
Urine, 8, 32-34, 58, 74

V

Vaccines, 41-43
Vagina
    bleeding, 9, 32, 74
    how to clean, 9
    pseudomenses, 9, 32, 74
    white discharge, 9
Vitamin D, 16, 21
Vitamin K, 4-5
Vitamins, 4-5, 16, 21, 88
Vomiting, 17, 36, 43, 48, 55,
    74-75

W

Water, 14, 16, 21, 23, 26, 31, 39,
    48
Weight gain, 5, 38
Weight loss, 5, 48

Y

Yeast diaper rash, 10, 59, 88
Yellow poop, 29-30

About The Author

Dr. Carole Keim MD (formerly Gedenberg) is a board-certified pediatrician from Boulder, CO.

She received an undergraduate degree in Biology at Colorado College, and went to medical school at Palacky University in the Czech Republic. She spent one month of surgical training in Finland, and three months as a medical volunteer in Argentina. She has spent the past decade broadening her medical knowledge by studying holistic, complementary and alternative medicine.

Dr. Keim worked as a family practice intern in Southern Colorado before completing her pediatric residency at Nassau University Medical Center (a large trauma center) in East Meadow, NY.

After residency, Dr. Keim worked in Pediatric Urgent Care in Lindenhurst, NY before moving back home to Boulder, CO to start a private practice. Her practice is called Doctor At Your Door LLC, and she makes house calls for pediatric patients 0-18 years old who live within half an hour of Boulder, CO. She also teaches Western Pathology to students at the Southwest Acupuncture College.

Dr. Keim is fluent in Spanish and Czech and is a black belt in taekwondo. In her free time, she enjoys knitting, crocheting, playing piano, and spending quality time with her family. She lives in Boulder, CO with her husband and children.

Free bookmark!

Tear out the next page and fold in half.

Reasons to call a doctor ASAP:

Rectal temperature >100.4 degrees, jaundice (yellow skin/eyes), apnea (not breathing), cyanosis (blue color around lips and on hands/feet), umbilical cord infection (redness spreading on the skin around the cord, sometimes with smelly discharge), diarrhea, choking, seizure, any head injury, fall from a height of 2 feet or more, blood in the diaper (except newborn girls can get a false period around day 5-7 and that is normal).

normal
poop
colors:

normal
urine
colors:

| "rusty pipes" day 1-3 | darker urine also day 1-3 |

baby's
stomach
size:

1 day old
5-7 ml
1-1.4 tsp

2 days old
22-27 ml
0.75-1 oz

1 week old
45-60 ml
1.5-2 oz

1 month old
80-150 ml
2.5-5 oz